MY TURN

WOMEN'S SEARCH FOR SELF AFTER THE CHILDREN LEAVE

MY TURN

WOMEN'S
SEARCH
FOR SELF
AFTER THE
CHILDREN
LEAVE

PATRICIA GOTTLIEB SHAPIRO

Peterson's
Princeton, New Jersey

About Peterson's

Peterson's is the country's largest educational information/communications company, pro-
viding the academic, consumer, and professional communities with books, software, and
on-line services in support of lifelong education access and career choice. Well-known
references include Peterson's annual guides to private schools, summer programs, colleges
and universities, graduate and professional programs, financial aid, international study,
adult learning, and career guidance. Peterson's Web site at petersons.com is the only
comprehensive—and most heavily traveled—education resource on the Internet. The site
carries all of Peterson's fully searchable major databases and includes financial aid sources,
test-prep help, job postings, direct inquiry and application features, and specially created
Virtual Campuses for every accredited academic institution and summer program in the
U.S. and Canada that offers in-depth narratives, announcements, and multimedia features.

Visit Peterson's on the Internet at http://www.petersons.com

Permission to reprint the following excerpt is gratefully acknowledged:

"Women Enough" from *Fear of Fifty* by Erica Jong. Reprinted by
permission of HarperCollins Publishers, Inc.

Library of Congress Cataloging-in-Publication Data

Shapiro, Patricia Gottlieb.
    My turn : women's search for self after the children leave / by
Patricia Gottlieb Shapiro.
       p.   cm.
    Includes bibliographical references and index.
    ISBN 1-56079-946-3
    1. Parent and adult child. 2. Middle aged women—Psychology.
3. Self-actualization (Psychology) 4. Intergenerational relations.
I. Title.
HQ755.86.S53   1996
155.6'6—dc20   96-1318
                                                                CIP

Editorial direction by Carol Hupping   Composition by Gary Rozmierski
Production supervision by Bernadette Boylan   Creative direction by Linda Huber
Copyediting by Kathy Salazar   Interior design by Cynthia Boone
Proofreading by Marie Burnett

Printed in the United States of America

10 9 8 7 6 5 4 3 2 1

For Andrew and Margot

Other books by Patricia Gottlieb Shapiro:

Caring for the Mentally Ill
Women, Mentors, and Success (with coauthor)
A Parent's Guide to Childhood and Adolescent Depression

CONTENTS

If I am not for myself, who is for me? And when I am for myself, what am I? And if not now, when?

—Hillel, *The Talmud*

ACKNOWLEDGMENTS

The kernel of the idea for this book began with several conversations with good friends whose children had just left home. Through those friends and their networks, I reached the women whose stories became the heart of this book. I appreciate the time each woman gave me and the openness and honesty with which she shared her emotions and experiences. I want to thank Marilyn Fountain, Sheila Inden, Patty Lemer, Bea Leopold, and Katie O'Brien for their generosity with interview leads as well.

I owe a special thanks to Meg Blackstone, whose reflections and provocative questions inspired me to reshape my original proposal to view my subject from the fresh perspective of women's development. Carol Mann, my agent, believed in this project from the very beginning and supported me throughout. Carol Hupping, my editor at Peterson's, shared my vision and helped me find my voice and stay true to it, while gently prodding me to dig a little deeper, say a little more. She has been steadfast in her support. I'm also appreciative of the following mental health professionals for their insights: Evelyn Bassoff, Marjorie Bayersdorfer, Vivian Greenberg, Emily Hancock, and Peggy Tietz. On the technical side, I want to thank Sandi Gelfin and Karen Baitzel for transcribing my tapes and Andrew Shapiro for compiling my bibliography.

Many friends and colleagues contributed to this effort in important ways. For their friendship and encouragement, I want to thank Norma Bolden, Jane Brooks, Anne Cogen, Doris Feingold, and Paula Slomsky. My sister, Anne Gottlieb Angerman, has been generous with interview leads, insights, and support. The women in my writers' group also have been a source of encouragement, experienced know-how, and practical advice. Myra Eskin, Marian

My Turn

Sandmaier, and Pat Wisch read early drafts of all my chapters. Their feedback helped me refine my prose and sharpen my thinking; their faith in me and this project continuously sustained me.

Lastly, I'm grateful for the trust and respect my family gave me to have my say. It would have been impossible to write an honest book without involving the lives of my husband and children. I've tried to do this carefully and thoughtfully without invading their privacy. I hope Andrew and Margot will view the personal sections of this book as they were meant to be: a true and loving memoir of our letting go.

Words cannot express the appreciation I owe my husband, Dick. He never wavered in his faith in me, supporting me continuously by doing whatever he could to make my life easier while I was writing this book. Sounding board, psychoanalyst-in-residence, and confidante, Dick was always available to share my ups and downs.

INTRODUCTION

I originally considered calling this book *The Empty Nest*. This title would be accurate, to the point, and offer instant recognition of the subject matter, I reasoned at the time. As I began my research, however, I realized that this familiar phrase, in fact, was an inaccurate and outdated description of the period after our children leave home. Once I embarked on the interviewing process, I realized further that my original title was also depressingly and unrealistically negative. Empty connotes vacant, void, and barren. In contrast, women told me personal stories teeming with vitality and pleasure after their children left home.

I talked with a straitlaced psychologist who discovered her passion for Caribbean dancing after her daughter went to college; a teacher who yearned to sail for years who bought herself a sailboat; a homemaker who thought she had no talents yet opened a frozen yogurt business; and a social worker who finally gratified her craving to read novels uninterrupted in the evening. These were not women who felt empty, whose "nests" withered away without their children's presence. These were vibrant women who felt that they had been given a new lease on life, a second chance at self-fulfillment without the encumbrances and responsibilities of children at home.

As I listened carefully to these women, searching for their motivation and the impetus for change, I heard one constant refrain: "It's *my* turn now." Many of us were taught that we were selfish if we put our needs before those of others. Our children and husbands *should* come first. Yes, we had jobs and careers, but we shoved our priorities to the back burner, sometimes grudgingly and sometimes not, while we raised our children. A stockbroker who worked full-time, managed the household, and did all the cooking and housework for her family complained to me, "I was hard-pressed to have a *life* when the boys were home." This is not to say that she didn't take time to exercise at the gym or meet a friend for lunch or go shopping. But her schedule—*her life*—was usually arranged around her husband's and her sons' activities. Of course, exceptions to this pattern exist, particularly among women with demanding careers, but they are uncommon.

With her sons away at college, the stockbroker told me, "It's my turn." Generally, when women used this phrase it signified an opportunity to define themselves and their lives on their own terms and make their needs and desires a priority. Finally, they could put themselves first. Women told me they had not been aware that they had led such other-centered lives until their children left home. Some women, in fact, had considered others foremost for so long that when their children left, they weren't even sure what they wanted or how they wished to spend their time. As one woman said, "I know it's my turn, but I don't even know what it's my turn *for*."

Exactly what comprised "my turn" varied from woman to woman. For some, it began as a small shift, such as going to the movies with her sister or telling her husband she needed quiet time after work. For others, a major transformation occurred, such as starting a new business or completing an education. Women told me they simply yearned to do *what* they wanted *when* they wanted. "My turn" was an opportunity for self-nurturing, self-discovery, and renewal. It was a time to develop relationships, to discover new interests, to unearth latent talents or buried pleasures, to expand careers (or trash them), to find fresh avenues for creativity, and to pursue lifelong dreams.

I don't mean to imply, however, that these women abandoned their families—although one woman shared with me her fantasy of "running away from home" and starting over as an independent woman of fifty, unfettered by husband or kids! Nor did these women disregard their husbands' or children's feelings. Instead, they renegotiated their relationships slowly and thoughtfully so that they gave their own feelings and needs primacy. Some did leave their marriages; others strengthened them. Most worked out a different quality of relationship with their children as young adults who lived away from home. Many found that friends became more central to their lives.

These shifts in relationships and in priorities came gradually. Growth did not come overnight for anyone. Many women grappled for months—even years—to come to terms with their children's departure. Some had difficulty letting go emotionally. Others had to accept that they were not perfect parents and that their children had disappointed them. All of these issues had to be resolved before women could embrace their freedom. Yet even the women who arrived at a resolution about the shape and texture of their lives without children at home admitted that this was not a final decision. It was a commitment that worked *for now*, a segment of their life as a work in progress.

Hearing about other women's struggles reassured me, because I needed confirmation that my own experiences were normal and common. I had always enjoyed my freedom when our two children went to overnight camp, so I eagerly looked forward to their departure for college. Earlier separations had not been difficult for either them or me. I didn't anticipate any rumblings of the so-called "empty-nest syndrome" because I knew I had a full life—a good marriage, a rewarding career, lots of friends, hobbies—with or without children at home. When our son, Andrew, went to college, I felt few repercussions and enjoyed spending a year with only our daughter, Margot, at home.

Yet much to my surprise, when she left the following September, I felt an enormous void. While the intense feelings of longing lasted only a few weeks, waves of emptiness came and went. Sometimes the house seemed too still, and I longed for the chatter of an eighteen-year-old. At other times, I cherished the quiet and the ability to talk on the phone or read without interruption. I enjoyed a sense of liberation: I could make plans to meet friends for dinner or travel without feeling guilty that I was neglecting my parental duties. These fluid, conflicting feelings ebbed and flowed from week to week and sometimes from day to day or even within the same twenty-four hours.

What surprised me most was that my work did not and could not fill the vacuum in my life. I have been a writer for fifteen years, authored three books, wrote hundreds of feature articles. My work absorbs me and challenges me, yet when my children left, it wasn't "enough" to compensate for the loss. Many of the women I interviewed verbalized similar emotions. "It was almost like in getting your life and a career together you assumed that you'd have enough gratification in your work to fulfill you," said a woman who makes and sells her own jewelry. "Well, guess what? I've done it. It's not where it's at. I thought that when the children left, I'd have my career to make me happy. I love what I do but my career isn't what I thought it would be. It really was the parenting that was going to my heart."

When I shared my feelings with my friends, all professional women, they expressed similar emotions. Our discussions, while comforting in one sense, were also unsettling, because they raised more questions than answers for me. I wondered just how long these intense initial feelings lasted. After the first bout of emotions, then how do women feel? What helps some adjust, and what prevents others from doing so? Why *doesn't* work protect some of us, as we expected, at times like this? And how long does it take to truly capture "my turn"? I undertook this book not because I had answers to these questions but precisely because I was searching for them.

I headed to the library in pursuit of answers. Much to my surprise, I could find only a handful of books on the *end* of active parenting, yet hundreds exist about the *beginning* of parenting. *What to Expect When You're Expecting*, for example, had sold four million copies by early 1995, according to the *New York Times*. Every nuance of becoming a parent, from conception to delivery, and on being a parent, from infancy to adolescence, has been written about in minute detail. Yet the transition from active parenting to the postparental period has been ignored, denied, or reduced to a single, negative stereotype. I wondered why no one had written a book called *What to Expect When Your Children Leave Home*.

I now understand why such a dearth of information exists. Despite hundreds of books on parenting, our society does not truly value mothering. Employed mothers receive very little support in terms of on-site child care or parental leave policies. Society scorns women who choose to stay home with their children and criticizes them for doing "nothing." We exalt motherhood in the abstract but blame mothers when their children have problems. Through my interviews I came to appreciate anew how profoundly and deeply women connect to their children—whether or not they work outside the home. If society valued this bond, then our children's leave-taking would be recognized as a crucial watershed for women. It would be understood that it's necessary to come to terms with a major change in a critical relationship.

A paucity of information exists for another reason as well. Until recently, male researchers studied adult development and focused their research on their own lives. They accepted the male experience as universal and swept women under the general masculine rubric. In Daniel Levinson's landmark book *The Seasons of a Man's Life*, for example, he mentions parenting only in passing. Yet mothering is central to women's existence. Only recently have women begun to write about their own development, particularly their lives after their fiftieth birthdays. Books by Gail Sheehy, Germaine Greer, and Betty Friedan mark a new validation of women's midlife experience as unique and as worthy of research and respect.

My own interviews confirmed for me the complexity, variety, and fullness of women's experience at midlife. As women spoke to me, they wove together the strands of their lives. In addition to issues related to work and family, they discussed their experience with menopause, their celebration or denial of their fiftieth birthday, their thoughts about their own mortality, and their desire and struggle to find or recover the parts of themselves they lost in caring for their children. Serious and thoughtful, these discussions reaffirmed for me that women without children at home have never been more dynamic, determined, and powerful.

This is a book about the impact of children leaving home on women today. It strongly challenges the "empty-nest syndrome" stereotype by showing how and why our children's departure becomes a catalyst for change—not a cause of depression. It explores whether and how work, either paid or volunteer, makes a difference in women's adjustment to their children's leave-taking.

The book begins by examining why the postparenting period has been neglected as a significant stage in women's development. By looking at the reasons why theorists have neglected women in general and why society marginalizes older women in particular, we will come to understand why our children's departure has been treated as either a nonevent or a medical malady.

This is also a book about the powerful, passionate bond that links women to their children. One woman summed up how many felt when she said, "We women lose our hearts to our children," and then added, "How do you get your heart back into your body when your child leaves?" From talking about their earliest memories of mothering to discussing how motherhood changed them, women voice a range of emotions and expectations. They'll speak of their fears about their inability to protect their children and of their conflicting needs for connection and for autonomy. Only by appreciating the significance of this bond can we truly understand the impact of our children's departure.

Our children's leave-taking is a natural demarcation, a time when many women reflect and reassess how successful they feel as parents. Of course, our children are not finished products, yet with active parenting over, most of us have made our major contribution. Women who are disappointed in their children or their children's lifestyle or troubled by a son's or daughter's emotional problems often blame themselves for their children's current difficulties. This book helps women understand their mothering experience as one—but by no means the sole—influence on how their children turned out.

We'll also look at the losses, both conscious and unconscious, that women experience when their children leave home and explore why they need to mourn these losses before they can welcome their freedom. In that sense, this is also a book about letting go. We'll see how separating from sons differs from separating from daughters. We'll also talk with women who have difficulty letting go of any of their children and examine the reasons why. In addition, we'll explore some of the other variables that determine whether and how women let go emotionally of their children.

This is also a book about freedom: freedom *from* responsibilities and caregiving and freedom *to* explore one's life in the fullest sense of the word. Without children at home, many women wondered, "Who am I now?" They then asked the corollary question: "What am I going to do with the rest of my life?" We'll see how some women relished their freedom while for others, personal anxieties and fear of repercussions in their relationships held them back. We'll meet some courageous women who overcame these fears to achieve their goals.

This is very much a book about relationships. It is about how the dynamics of our significant relationships shift when our youngest child leaves home. We'll see how women learned to relate differently to their children as young adults and how they struggled to carve out a role in their grown children's lives. We'll explore how the children's departure influenced marital relationships and friendships. And we'll hear how women grappled to balance their desire for intimacy with their need for independence in their intimate relationships.

Throughout the entire book, women will reflect on how their work impacts in different ways on their lives without children at home. Is work a substitute for a child or a buffer against loss? Does work protect women from feeling the brunt of their children's departure, or is it simply a diversion, a way to avoid facing issues and feelings? And does a woman's response to her children's departure differ depending on whether her work is a passion that gives her an identity, a nine-to-five job that provides a needed paycheck, or a volunteer project?

Lastly, this is a book about possibilities. It is about making changes in our relationships, in ourselves, and in our lives. It is about capturing our turns for whatever suits our fancy. You'll meet women just like you and me who have rediscovered themselves and transformed their lives after their children left home. In the final chapter, you'll gain the perspective and the practical tools you need to begin the process of seizing your turn.

I approached my subject matter and gathered information for this book wearing several hats. My education and training as a clinical social worker informed this project, as it does all my work. As a writer deeply interested in understanding women's issues, I studied material on women's development, midlife women, separation and loss, and mothering and motherhood. But the true impetus for this project came from my need as a woman and a mother to validate my own experiences and feelings.

My friends' reactions had reassured me, but I needed to get beyond my narrow circle of upper-middle-class professional women to see whether our feelings were universal. Were we representative of most women with careers? And if we, who had such full lives, felt this way, how did others feel? Women with jobs, not satisfying careers? Those who did not work outside the home? I needed to know that my experiences were normal for women whose last child had left home. I sensed I was embarking on a new phase of my life; I wanted to share my experiences and to understand and learn from other women.

This book is not meant to be a scientific study but an in-depth exploration of the postparenting period. I did not use a random sample; quantifying information was not my goal. I wanted to hear from a wide range of women speaking in their own voices. Their concerns, their fears, their hopes and their dreams, I knew, would be powerfully conveyed in their own words.

My Turn

To draw conclusions that would represent a cross section of women, I knew I needed a broad-based sample. I began the interviewing process by contacting friends and acquaintances all over the country and telling them that I was writing a book on how women adjust after their children leave home. They often responded with a knowing laugh, then spilled forth the names of friends and relatives who were either having "a rough time" or had done "amazing things" since their kids had left home. These women, in turn, referred me to other women, and the process snowballed. I did not interview anyone I knew personally. The interviews themselves lasted from 1 to 3 hours, and each interview was taped and transcribed. I rarely left an interview without the names of additional women with whom to speak.

The criteria for being interviewed were simple: all of a woman's children must have been out of the house for at least six weeks but not more than six years. I wanted to understand women's struggles and triumphs along this six-year span as well as talk with those at both ends of the process. That is, I wanted to tap those immediate, intense first feelings of loss, and I also wished to capture the gratification women felt when they had successfully built a full life without children at home. I used the six-year cutoff point because I believed that by five or six years most women have adjusted to their new status. I hoped that women who had been child-free longer would serve as role models for those still grappling with the newness of their children's departure.

Most of the women I interviewed had children who attended college or graduate school. Although most college-age children are financially dependent on their parents and still come home for vacations, they no longer live at home. For most women, active parenting ends when the youngest child goes to college. Women whose children have married or moved to another city after college, however, told me that this later transition was far more difficult because the separation felt more permanent. This study did not focus on that transition, however.

I interviewed forty-five women from all parts of the country: city, suburban, and rural women; women who were married, divorced, separated, and widowed; professional women and those from working-class families; and women of varied religious and cultural backgrounds. Ninety percent were white women; about 10 percent, African Americans. They ranged in age from 45 to 60. I changed each woman's name as well as her city and place of employment to protect her privacy. With few exceptions, I did not change their occupations. All the quotations you'll read are verbatim.

Eighty percent of my sample worked outside the home, and 20 percent were primarily homemakers. The employed women were social workers, decorators, teachers, secretaries, manufacturer's reps, nurses, psychologists, attorneys, and business owners. I had almost finished the interviewing process when I realized that I had interviewed no corporate women. I went back to my sources. I contacted women in corporations and well-placed women who know women in corporations. Very few names surfaced of women who met my criteria. As I pieced together the information I received from these sources, I realized the reasons that I could find few corporate women in management whose children had been out of the house from six weeks to six years: Many women from ages 45 to 60 either don't have children—they sacrificed families and sometimes marriage for their careers—or they postponed getting pregnant, so their children are younger and still at home.

Consequently, you'll find few corporate women profiled in these pages. If you work in a corporation yourself, however, you will still find countless women whose stories will resonate with your own. Careers aside, we all share many emotions and experiences as well as hopes and dreams.

As I worked on this book, writing at the computer, reviewing transcripts, listening to other women's stories about their children's departure, I often thought about my own experience after our children left home. Of course, each person's situation is unique. Yet when I heard certain themes emerge again and again—those of loving and letting go, acceptance, valuing and nurturing ourselves—I couldn't help making connections with my own life. Some women gave me support. Others motivated me. Many inspired me. I fervently hope that the women whose stories you'll read in this book will serve as models for you too. I also hope that their stories will inspire you and embolden you to make shifts in your relationships, to take risks in your lives, and to recapture the parts of yourself you may have lost while you raised your children.

That's what this book is about. It is about freedom and discovery, possibility and promise. It is about seizing our turns.

CHAPTER ONE

A NEGLECTED PASSAGE

It is 6:30 p.m. My husband, Dick, and I are eating pizza on the porch. A rare evening in October—it is warm enough to sit outside with just a sweater. Around us, the leaves, in reds and yellows, fall gently to the ground. A Mozart piano concerto plays on the radio. We're chatting. After about ten minutes, we run out of conversation and continue eating silently.

My Turn

A tranquil scene surrounds us, but inside I am churning: *Is this it? Is this what I've been waiting for? Is this what I have to look forward to for the next thirty years?*

The stillness sits between us like a wedge. My mind draws a blank: What can we talk about tonight? I wish the phone would ring. The refrigerator looks like a bachelor's: a gallon of milk, a carton of o.j., an opened bottle of Chardonnay, a hunk of Jarlsberg, and a head of romaine. Why bother to cook for two people? We finish dinner in 20 minutes. Then, what? I can't remember where our evenings went before. Margot, our daughter, spent so little time at home her senior year of high school, yet somehow knowing she'd be home or checking in made a difference. Our son, Andrew, had gone to school the previous September.

Although I did not consciously prepare myself for Margot's departure, I remember taking a mental inventory of my life the summer before she went to school. I came away feeling that I had the ingredients for a full life—even with the children away. I had a career as a freelance writer and book author, a good marriage, close friends, hobbies, and interests. Separations from my children had not been difficult for me in the past.

Yet I must have had some inkling that everything might not be just fine after Margot left, because I had carefully orchestrated the six weeks after Dick and I took her to school in Washington State. On the way home, I stopped in Denver to visit my sister for a few days and then went on to attend a writer's conference in Aspen. I came home to a packed schedule of speaking engagements and writing assignments. I met friends for dinner whenever I felt like it, went to the movies during the week, and took off with Dick for the weekend on a whim.

But by October, the flurry of activity had died down. I had grown tired of running around. Much as I enjoyed my newfound freedom, I knew that my racing around was an attempt to avoid facing a big, empty house in the suburbs.

The house, still and silent, symbolized the void I felt within me. A huge chunk of my life had been gouged out. I wasn't sure what remained of me. Was I still a mother once the kids were gone? How would my relationship with them change? The realization that my active parenting had ended prompted other soul-searching questions: What was I going to do with all my time and energy? How could I now live my life in a meaningful way? Who was I, anyway? With the children gone, everything seemed different. I began to look through a new lens at my marriage, my parenting, my aging, my career, and my very life itself.

I didn't feel the out-and-out depression attributed to stay-at-home moms. But I felt out of sorts and rootless. These feelings threw me for a loop. No one told me I'd feel this way. Instead I had heard about how liberated women felt with their children gone, that this was such a happy, carefree time. Besides, I hadn't lived solely for my children. I had a career, I had an identity as a writer, I was a person beyond mommy. I thought my career would make me feel better or at least buffer some of my feelings. It didn't really temper my feelings, but it served as a diversion: When I threw myself into a writing project, I did forget for a while. But no matter how engrossing, work could not fill that void.

At the time, I thought I was the only one not ecstatic after her children had left home. Every time I ran into another empty nester, she'd greet me with the same expectant question: "Isn't it wonderful with the kids gone?" The short, superficial answer: Yes, parts of it were wonderful. The house stays clean and neat. I can buy a bag of chocolate chocolate-chip cookies and find them in the same place a day later. I can listen to classical music all evening without hearing strains of rock blaring from upstairs. And I sleep much more soundly. But beneath those superficial advantages stirred that cauldron of emotions that I didn't expect.

When I shared my feelings with close friends, they were relieved to get beyond cocktail party chatter to talk frankly about how they were coping with their children out of the house. One began frantically house-hunting to fill the void. Another, an artist, spent the first weekend after her son left crying and cleaning his room, then began preparing for the first solo show of her work. A third, a management consultant, went into psychotherapy to try to comprehend the despair she felt. They all found different ways to contend with the changes that the departure of their children wrought.

As I interviewed the women who comprised my research for this book, I realized that many, many women shared these feelings. One woman, who has a thriving business as an antique appraiser, said, "If I had to describe how I felt honestly, I guess I was 'a half,' parenting was 'a quarter,' and being a wife was 'a quarter.' So it made me 'a whole.' Do you know what I mean? It made me 'a one.' Now with the kids gone, there's 'a quarter' gone, so now I'm not 'a whole' anymore." Another woman, a psychotherapist, said she felt "lost" from the moment she dropped her last child off at college. Her car broke down on the way home and that for her symbolized her family falling apart.

Other women used vivid imagery to describe the intensity of their initial feelings after their youngest child left home. One woman said she felt like her arm had been amputated. In contrast, another said she and her husband were "drunk with the freedom. We were eating out every night. We were going to movies after work. We did not know what to do with ourselves, we were *so* excited."

Whether they felt excited or bereft, liberated or sad, or all of these emotions at different times, as many did, women told me that the depth of their feelings signaled that *something* was changing. At the time, they weren't quite sure what. And during those initial months, I, too, felt confused about what I was experiencing. I sensed I was embarking on a new phase of my life, but I wasn't sure just what that entailed. I now know that we faced a critical juncture. With the children out of the house, we were entering what sociologists call the "postparental period": a phase of loss and liberation, of reflection and reassessment, of challenge and action. A phase rich with possibility.

A NEGLECTED STAGE

The period after our children leave home has been neglected as a significant stage of women's life cycle. It has been recognized only in a negative way as the "empty nest" period. The notion that only we *women*—and not our husbands—suffer from "the empty-nest syndrome" when our children leave home further demeans us. The symptoms, or signs, of our "disease" supposedly parallel those of clinical depression: profound sadness and despair, sleeplessness, loss of appetite and sexual desire, and an inability to experience pleasure in daily life. The concept implies that we have only one function: to breed and raise our children. When our children leave, so the theory goes, we feel so purposeless and our lives so meaningless that we become clinically depressed.

The "empty-nest syndrome" became popularized after research in the 1960s found that women became depressed after their children left home.[1] The public did not know, however, that these studies were done on women hospitalized for depression. The press and the public generalized from these results as though the women studied represented run-of-the-mill Mrs. Middle Americas. Thus, a stereotype developed that had little basis in truth for the majority of middle-aged women. And the term "empty-nest syndrome," often used interchangably with empty nest, has become part of our cultural language. Explanations are no longer necessary—we all know what it means.

Even research to the contrary has not quelled the stereotype. Lillian Rubin, for example, interviewed 160 midlife women for her 1979 book, *Women of a Certain Age*. Rather than finding them depressed, she wrote, "Almost all the women I spoke with respond to the departure of their children, whether actual or impending, with a decided sense of relief."[2] A 1980 study of 3,000 adults found that empty nesters were *less* depressed than those living with children or those who never had children.[3] Other research studies have been inconsistent about whether women become depressed when their children leave home. Yet the concept has become so ingrained in our culture that challenging it still makes headlines. In 1995, the *Philadelphia Inquirer* reported that a British study concluded that the "empty-nest syndrome" is a myth.[4]

That the period after children leave home has been perceived negatively or disregarded totally bespeaks a larger issue: how our society views older women. I had often heard about how middle aged (and older) women feel invisible, yet I had never experienced it until I stood in line at the post office one day, about six months after my fiftieth birthday. In front of me stood a young woman wearing jeans and a tee shirt who looked about 18 years old. Behind me waited another young woman who looked about the same age wearing khakis and a denim shirt. They recognized each other and started playing catch-up, talking around me. "What are you doing now?" asked the one in jeans. "I'm finishing law school," answered the other, showing her a pile of envelopes, "applying for jobs. What about you?"

"I'm applying for social work school. I want to go to Smith, but I'm also considering Penn," she answers.

Hearing she's interested in social work school, I pipe up, "Oh, I went to Penn School of Social Work." She nods, her eyes glaze over. "Twenty-five years ago," I add, laughing. She forces a smile, looks down at her letters. End of conversation.

At first I wondered why she didn't ask me about my experience. Then I realized that she doesn't care; she thinks my experience is irrelevant to hers. Most middle-aged women can tell similar tales of feeling transparent. The media characterizes women beyond 50 as eccentric frumps or doddering idiots, unless it airbrushes them to youthful perfection or omits them altogether from the script. Yet men over 50 are considered wise, charming, and sexy. Consider an ad for Paul Newman's 1995 movie, *Nobody's Fool*. Reported to be 70, Newman appears close-up in profile: suntanned, gray hair cropped short, crow's feet crinkling around his alert blue eyes, mouth slightly open, poised for action. The caption, "Worn to Perfection," implies that he gets more perfect as he ages. Have you ever seen a similar ad for a female movie star over 50?

Movie critics and middle-aged female stars often lament that few strong roles for women exist once they pass midlife; book reviewers often have similar complaints. When Germaine Greer researched *The Change*, her book about menopause, she reported that she could find very few middle-aged women in fiction. She writes, "All our heroines are young. Even women writers who are themselves 50 or over write about young women. Barbara Cartland, who is over 90, has written more than 550 books, but I doubt that one of them has a heroine over 25. Older women themselves suffer from youthism and contribute to the prejudice against themselves; they endure the never-ending gibes against menopausal women, against mothers-in-law, against crones in general, without a word of protest."[5]

When Greer complained to another middle-aged woman that no one wrote novels about them, she said, "Oh, that's because nothing happens to us." Greer concludes that "If there is a belief that nothing happens to middle-aged women, it is only because middle-aged women do not talk about what does happen to them."[6] Perhaps they don't talk because no one asks or listens to what they have to say.

Of the forty-five middle-aged women I interviewed for this book, nearly all had "something" happen to them. They welcomed an opportunity to talk and had plenty to say. I spoke with Jane Morris, an attractive, vibrant 45-year-old homemaker who bought a frozen yogurt franchise after her son and daughter went to college. She told me how she purposely chose a business open only six months a year, because, she said, "I like to do a lot of things. It's almost like I don't want to give up my *life* for work. I do want to have a purpose, and I do want to achieve something, but I like to be with my friends. I like to garden. I like to go out with my dogs and just walk. I just don't want to spend my whole life in a job and at the end of twenty-five years, they give you a watch, and you wonder what the hell you did it for. Forget this.

"Now that I'm older and have more freedom, I want to work for *me*, and I'm not afraid to take risks as when the kids were little, because Tom and I can always move to a townhouse or an apartment, and we'll still live. If everything hits the road, who cares?"

Is this a woman to whom "nothing" happens? True, she had the means to fulfill her goals, but she reconsidered her priorities with the children gone, took chances, and acted assertively to achieve her objectives. In the business world, she noticed how others perceived her differently now that she was not "just a mother." She says, "For the first time in my life, I had businessmen trying to sell me things. It was like, I'm the president of this company, I have my own office, the whole bit. I don't feel different inside, but they perceived me to be different and treated me differently. In the past they'd probably call someone like me 'honey' just because she's walking around the mall with two kids trailing behind."

Jane's comments illustrate another reason why the effect on women of their children's departure has gone unrecognized: Our society depreciates mothers. While both men and women extol the joys of motherhood and the importance of family, when society measures a woman, motherhood doesn't hold a candle to work. What truly matters is how we make a living, not what we do at home. If motherhood were prized and respected, our children's departure would be recognized as significant for women.

COMPLEX, CONNECTED LIVES

Research on adult development, from the classic studies to the more contemporary, emphasizes the importance of separation. Yet connections and relationships are more crucial to women's lives than separation. The reason for this discrepancy? The studies focus on the lives of men and use the male model to represent all human development—another instance of how women have been ignored and devalued from the end of the nineteenth century to the present. Carl Jung first suggested that people continue to evolve into adulthood. A disciple of Sigmund Freud's, Jung broke with Freud because Jung felt Freud focused too narrowly on childhood development and its influence on adult problems.[7] Erik Erikson, however, deserves credit for dividing the entire life cycle, not just childhood, into eight equally important life stages, which he called the "Eight Stages of Man."[8] As his title suggests, he took the male experience and developed a universal theory from it.

In more contemporary theory, psychologist Daniel Levinson, author of the seminal book *The Seasons of a Man's Life*, discovered and created a psychosocial theory of human life, considered the first such "empirically based conceptual breakthrough" since Erikson's.[9] Levinson divided the life cycle into five twenty-year intervals called eras, each of which consists of alternative periods of stability and transition. According to Levinson, the eras in men's lives follow one another in a predictable, orderly sequence, give or take a few years. He organized his study around men's career development. Although he discusses the importance of relationships for men's growth, these relationships matter primarily in the way in which they support a man and his career. For example, in describing a man's wife, Levinson writes, "The special woman is like the true mentor: her special quality lies in her connection to the young man's Dream. . . . she shares it, believes in him as its hero, gives it her blessing, joins him on the journey and creates a 'boundary space' within which his aspirations can be imagined and his hopes nourished."[10]

Women lead far more complex, varied, and unpredictable lives than men. Women usually organize their lives around their relationships with their significant others, not around their work. Before they make a career move, most women evaluate how it affects their personal life: on their decision to have children, postpone pregnancy, or find child care, and on their husband (if they have one) and his needs. Unlike men's more linear work course, women's usually consists of starts, stops, meanders, interruptions, revisions, and detours as they accommodate the others in their lives.

Consider the variations in women's lives just during their twenties. Some women marry but hold off having children so they can concentrate on their careers; others marry and decide to have children right away but choose the mommy track so they stay connected with their field. Others decide to remain single in their twenties, establish themselves in their career, and postpone marriage and children until later. Still others pursue marriage, children, and career or job simultaneously and equally vigorously.

Although Levinson acknowledges the importance of fatherhood to men, it is not a major theme of his book. No references to parenting or fatherhood exist in the index nor does he capture the essence of a father's relationship with his children. Motherhood, however, is one of the key themes of most women's lives—whether or not they choose to remain childless, are biological mothers, or are currently caring for children.

Levinson believes that as men age, they strive to become more independent and autonomous.[11] Women develop differently, however. Feminist writers, such as Carol Gilligan and Jean Baker Miller, believe that women fuse the two tasks of forming an identity and developing intimate relationships and develop our identity while in relationships with others.[12] That is, we develop in a context of relationships with others and gain our sense of self through making and then maintaining relationships.

Building on Gilligan's and Miller's work, researchers and clinicians at the Stone Center for Developmental Services and Studies at Wellesley College have developed an alternative to most of the existing theories, which, like Levinson's, posit some form of autonomy or separation as the goal of development. Their "self-in-relation" model seems more fitting for women's development. They see connection with others as a key element of action and growth, not as a means to self-enhancement as Levinson's theory implies.[13] This theory seems truer and closer to most women's experience: that we develop our sense of self not in isolation but through relationships, through being an "other," and we grow and develop within the context of attachments. (I believe this holds true for men also, but to admit this would create too much discomfort for men, because they would see themselves as too dependent, particularly on women.)

This theory, however, has an undercurrent: that *because* most of us grew up conditioned to consider others before ourselves, we often feel selfish when we make our needs primary. When our children leave home, we have an opportunity to put ourselves first. That doesn't mean that relationships matter less to us. But for once, *we* can become the priority—if we so choose. Yet many of us have difficulty giving ourselves permission to do this. Sandy Sherman is someone who has struggled with the notion of selfishness. A researcher with two sons in their twenties, she welcomed her second son's departure because she'd have more time for herself, yet couldn't help thinking that others may view her choices as selfish. She told me, "When Ray left, I was sad and excited for him, but I had some trepidation about what it would mean for me. I had read about the empty nest," she laughs. "My life did change remarkably. And it was wonderful, but I felt very different. I felt older. I had no kids at home. And that turned out to be a wonderful, liberating experience, but it was a unique and particular developmental period for me as an adult."

What was it like for her? "I was feeling that I would get my life back. For twenty-two years, I had been their mother. We lived in Ohio for ten years, and on that street, where we lived, I was Ray's and Steve's mother, Tom's wife, and Nippy's and Snippy's (the two dogs) mother. Then I worked part-time in the mayor's office, and I ran a catering business with a friend. I certainly had an identity, but I was really hard pressed to have a life."

Why did Sandy feel that she didn't have "a life"? On one level, her days teemed with activity and busyness. Certainly, she had roles: as a mother, a wife, and a working woman. But she didn't feel that it was *her* life, that she was her own person. Her needs and desires were satisfied only after everyone else in the family was taken care of. Sandy's comments were typical of many of the women I interviewed.

When Ray left, Sandy says, "I got my life back." She joined two book clubs, constantly went out to dinner with friends, and took a course on spirituality with her husband. The frenetic activity lasted about six months. Sandy now acknowledges that she had to test the limits of her freedom. Three years later, she has settled into a life without children that pleases her. She explains, "I come home (from work), and I love being in the house by myself. It's very selfish. I am more selfish than I ever was. And only selfish with my time, not with my interest or with my enthusiasm. But I'm much more protective of my time, for me to do what I want. Which mostly means being alone and reading. And if people think I'm strange, I just shrug my shoulders and say, 'Yeah, well, I'm strange.'"

Anyone who has lived with children knows the difficulty of finding quiet time to sit alone and read a good novel. Such a simple pleasure hardly seems selfish, yet it takes time for many of us to feel comfortable putting ourselves first, particularly if we have internalized society's messages about selfishness.

THE AGING CONNECTION

Contrary to the work of male developmentalists and despite a culture that marginalizes older women, the postparental period is important for us because of its link to our aging. Our children leaving home marks the loss of our youth. Active parenting has ceased. The "young mother with school-aged children at home" label no longer fits. Whether we admit it or not, we have become middle-aged women with young adult children. We have crossed the line and entered a different, older age bracket.

We often perceive our own aging—or lack of it—in the context of others'. As I get older, I notice how other people show their age and I can't help comparing myself to them. Who's aging better? Who's aging well? Where do I fit in? This may seem competitive, but I've also lost a sense of what the numbers mean. Those two young women in the post office looked 18 to me, but they were closer to 25. On the other hand, when Gloria Steinem said, "This is what 60 looks like," she acknowledged that society's concept of aging, or 60 in particular, has changed. Sixty is no longer considered old. Today, Gloria Steinem represents 60: slim, attractive, articulate, and vibrant.

My husband and I had the following conversation driving home from a birthday party for a friend whom we hadn't seen in five years:

Pat: David has really aged.

Dick: Yeah, he looks so old.

Pat: How much older than you is he?

Dick: Only two years.

Pat: He looks much older. He's hunched over. You look about ten years younger.

Dick: Yeah, and he got fat.

The conversation goes round and round as we compare our appearances to other people's at the party. When we get home, we get "comfortable." I take off my new pants outfit, wipe off my makeup and throw on old sweats. Dick puts on his faded khakis and a sweatshirt. I joke, "Next we'll take out our teeth."

We laugh but underneath the humor lies the realization that we are aging—albeit well for now. Thinking about the party, I realized that I didn't feel like I fit in. Everyone else seemed older, more mature and middle-aged, than I. I'm reminded of my grandmother, who at 85 years of age didn't want to move to a nursing home because she didn't want to live with "all those old people." Perhaps I'm in denial too.

But I don't think so. For most of the women I interviewed, their children leaving home alerted them: I'm at a different stage now; I'm older. Some, who do seem in denial, greeted my questions about their aging with a flip reply: "Aging is not a big deal," or "Fifty is just a number," or "I don't think about it. I just do what I have to do."

The more introspective women, however, grappled with the sense that time now has a different meaning. Barbara Bennett, an articulate, blunt-spoken woman who publishes a weekly newspaper in the Midwest, told me, "I feel like time is racing. I can't even hold it fast enough in my hands. It seems like mercury dripping through my hands. You think that you have a handle on it, and it just spurts away from you. I can somehow remember when I was a kid that summer seemed so long and so wonderful, sitting around and swinging and sucking on honeysuckle and playing in the street all the time. Stuff like that. I just don't have that feeling even though I get good pockets of leisure time. And since this is my own business, I can choose when I want to do things. But I feel that I am really racing now toward a decline.

"I never took a vacation away from my kids. Maybe that was stupid, but it just never seemed like such a big deal for me. I liked being with my kids, and we didn't have babysitters that often. I feel like I am making up for that lost time now."

Although she knows that she *can't* make up for lost time, Barbara tries to pack a lot into her days now. She realizes too that time has become finite. She *won't* postpone that trip to the islands with her husband. She *will* take the computer course this winter. Somewhere around midlife, we all realize that we won't live forever. We see contemporaries, our friends, diagnosed with cancer, keeling over from heart attacks on NordicTracks. We may not talk about mortality as such, but we do things that show that we think about it. If we can afford them, some of us buy condos at the seashore or cabins in the mountains to truly enjoy the remaining years without children underfoot. Others go cross country in RVs or move closer to their grandchildren.

The media called us the sandwich generation, because we cared for our aging parents and raised our growing children at the same time. Now many of us face our parents' frailties, as well as their deaths. When they die, we become aware that no one will protect us any longer. No more safety nets exist: We are next in line. As we struggle to accept the loss of our parents, our children leave home—another rug pulled from under us. With our parents gone or failing *and* our children out of the house, we face our ultimate aloneness. Divorced women and widows feel this particularly keenly.

Menopause, too, forces us to confront our mortality. We are no longer young, fertile, fecund. Our childbearing years are over. Do we grieve or rejoice? I believe that every woman mourns this loss on some level, whether consciously or unconsciously. The majority of the women I interviewed, however, told me they would not want to repeat their childrearing years. Once was enough. Their primary conscious feeling today was plain, old-fashioned relief. They did not want to dwell on the negatives of menopause; they had far more important, positive issues to talk about. They were either taking hormones or not; experiencing hot flashes and mood swings or not; miserable but coping or just coping. Most of my interviewees saw menopause as a necessary part of life but in no way a deterrent to achieving their goals or moving on with their lives.

Women found the outward signs of aging harder to ignore, however. These reminded them every day that they were getting older. Women told me of suddenly not recognizing their own face in the mirror. "My age hits me when I look in the mirror. I am surprised every time. You would think that I would be used to it by now," said an attorney. How does she remember herself? "At some point where I don't have to diet, and I am thinner, and I look younger. I'm still expecting that face to be in the mirror. And it isn't. I go around with that younger picture in my head and when I say, 'I'm 54,' it seems absolutely improbable. I do not feel 54. Fifty-four is old."

Others spoke of an even greater fear: looking in the mirror and seeing their mothers. A college professor decided to get a chemical peel on her upper lip, not because she hated the hundreds of tiny lines but because they reminded her of her mother. I remember looking in the mirror one morning after a particularly rough sleepless night and seeing my mother's (and my grandfather's) bags under my eyes. I was horrified. Even though I know I inherited them, their presence signified that I was getting older. And getting older *like my mother*. Like the college professor, I feared that I would become my mother and all the traits I hated about her would visit me in my later years.

The youngest child often leaves home close to a woman's fiftieth birthday, and she's hit with a double whammy. Whether she perceives the half-century milestone as a loss or liberation depends on how she feels about her life around the time of her birthday. Paula Wilson, an affable, fun-loving woman who has been married to a businessman for twenty-five years, told me that she didn't want to celebrate or even acknowledge her birthday. With her husband's business smarts and the recent launching of her own interior decorating studio, she thought they'd be financially independent when she hit 50, but things have not turned out as she hoped. With much emotion, she said: "I don't want to be 50. I am devastated. I want a face-lift. I want an eye-lift. This is not a happy time. I don't want to be 50. Don't give me a party. I don't want one. I don't feel like celebrating.

"Everyone says the fifties are a great age, but it's hard now to be 50 and have less money than when you were 40. I thought by now that I wouldn't have to work and that I could just do whatever I wanted. It has not turned out that way. That's a big disappointment. I thought we'd be on our way to financial independence, and instead, I'm worried about our retirement."

Paula is bitter and disillusioned: Her life has not turned out as she expected or as she fantasized. Her negative frame of mind cast a pall over her fiftieth birthday. Yet other women who have far less in the way of possessions or relationships have chosen to celebrate this milestone.

Sarah West, a San Francisco psychotherapist, approached her fiftieth birthday with an entirely different mind-set. A soft-spoken woman who shares her feelings easily, she told me of the losses she endured during the eighteen months prior to her birthday: her husband died of cancer, a heart attack killed her father, and her daughter, her only child, left for college on the East Coast. "Coming after all the losses and all the grieving and everything, turning 50 was . . . I had more of a feeling that I'm a survivor," she said. "Screw it, I made it this far. What lies ahead? It was more a chance to celebrate."

Sarah invited eight of her closest friends over. In her studio dimly lit with candles, she undressed, and they each massaged a part of her body and held her and sang lullabies and childhood songs to her. Then they each performed a special dance to her. The celebration concluded with a vegetarian feast. She says, "It was beautiful. It was something I could never reproduce. I only did it because I was at the end of myself. I felt like I was going to die. I was raw and fragile from the losses. So turning 50 was for me a liberation." Sarah could have withdrawn from others and wallowed in her sorrow. Instead, she reached out for help, and her friends responded.

A TIME OF GROWTH

Everyone knows that for children to mature and become independent, they must leave home and separate from their parents. But few recognize the reverse: that this separation is necessary for a woman's growth and development as well. For this reason alone, the postparental period is a significant stage in our development.

A passionate, powerful bond links us to our children. This complex, complicated connection abounds with pleasure as well as with angst. Our feelings about motherhood and about how we mother run deep, irrespective of how we live our lives. Those of us who work outside the home don't feel this passion any less than full-time homemakers do. From the time we feel the first kick in utero and listen to our baby's heartbeat through the obstetrician's stethoscope on our bellies, we bond indelibly to our children.

When the children leave, where does our passion go? *To wherever our hearts lead us.* We can now unearth pleasures lain dormant, rediscover childhood interests, develop hobbies long forgotten, push our intellectual limits, find our spiritual selves, and pursue political or social agendas. Margaret Mead called it postmenopausal zest, that creativity and energy released when we no longer need to care for children. Contrary to the 1960s research on the "empty-nest syndrome," recent studies have shown that the last child leaving creates *conditions of change*, which show increasing impact as women move through this period. Most women experience an increase in activity, excitement, overall happiness, and pride and a decrease in depression.[14]

For the first time in many years, our choices have no external boundaries: We can throw away that internal stopwatch that marked schooltime, dinnertime, bedtime.[15] The constraints now are internal: old parental tapes, societal dictates, and personal fears and anxieties. These can be enormously inhibiting, as we'll see later when we examine our choices and the difficulties we face in achieving our goals. Yet despite our struggles and our longing to recapture parts of our past, very few of us would give up our new freedom. Why? "It's my turn now," echoed woman after woman.

IT'S MY TURN

I'm probably typical of women raised in the '50s and '60s. I married at 25 in 1969, had my son in '72 and my daughter in '74. Even though I didn't devote myself exclusively to raising the children, my family always came first. I married on the cusp of the women's movement, so it had little effect on my early marriage. My husband put in long hours in his business and enjoyed playing with the children when he came home, but I had the major responsibility for child care, cooking, and the house. In contrast, my sister, who is four years younger and married in '75, grabbed hold of the movement's stance on equality and made it the *modus operandi* of her family life. A member of the "me" generation, she follows the philosophy that says, "I'll do what's best for me, because if I'm happy, the whole family will be happy."

I always worked, except for six months after Andrew was born. I had part-time jobs as a social worker and a writer when the children were young and, later, a full-time career as a freelance writer and author. But I always made sure a home-cooked dinner graced the table at 6 p.m., the kids were driven to gymnastics or baseball practice, the wash was done, and the refrigerator stocked. When the children attended grade school, I stopped writing at 3:00 so I'd be available for them. Yet I didn't put my life on hold either. I volunteered in the children's schools and in my synagogue, took courses at the local night school, did aerobics and fast-walked with friends, played tennis in the summer, and enjoyed weaving in the winter. I had a full and varied life. *But I never came first.* The family always took top priority.

Yet when I raised our children, I didn't feel diminished or devalued. It wasn't as though I were a frustrated concert pianist forced to put my career on hold for eighteen years while I raised our kids. I *chose* this life. Of course, I chose it in the cultural context in which I lived. I received specific messages from my parents and from society: Find a husband, get married, have kids, and possibly have a "little" career—naturally, teaching or social work—to fall back on "in case anything should happen." (Translation: should my husband die suddenly; divorce was less common in the late '60s.)

My experience may seem outdated and irrelevant to the high-powered attorney working 80 hours a week, but we have more in common than at first glance. The reality in terms of who does child care and housework differs little today from when I raised our children. Sixty-five percent of women with children under 18 years of age are in the labor force.[16] Yet they still have the major responsibility for child care, housework, cooking, and cleaning.[17]

Today's baby boomers often navigate their hectic lives with blinders on, narrowly focused on two parallel tracks: work and family, their dual priorities. When their children leave, one track will be empty. These women will then confront the same issues I faced when our children left home, because for most of us—unless our work is truly a passion—motherhood is our highest priority. That's what I found among a majority of women I interviewed. And a study of 232 college-educated, married women confirmed my contention. It found that *all the women*, whose ages ranged from 46 to 61, said being a wife and mother was their primary role, regardless of whether they had ever worked in the paid workforce.[18]

I fear that career-driven mothers may be *less* prepared for what lies ahead, because they may not realize the significance of motherhood to them and may think that their work will insulate them from feeling the repercussions of their children's departure. Certainly, they can throw themselves into their careers with new zeal and added energy when their children leave home. But if they are searching for balance, like many women at midlife, then devoting themselves 100 percent to their work may feel less than satisfying. Career women often do not have time to develop other interests or hobbies while raising their children. When their children leave, these women may feel more of a void initially—until they find ways to enrich their lives.

For some of the women in my study, work did insulate them. When their youngest child left, they threw themselves into their work with a vengeance. They worked longer hours, took on extra projects, became more involved. This involvement helped them avoid and postpone (sometimes indefinitely) facing feelings or issues that their children's leaving precipitated. But these women did not unearth passions or discover hidden talents after their children left. These women reported to me that "nothing changed" when their last child left home. Even though their children no longer lived with them, the women continued living pretty much the same way, except that work took up a larger chunk of their time. Others—including myself—found that work, while crucial to our well-being, could not fill the void after our children left home. As I reflected on my interviews in light of my library research, I realized that those who experienced the most discomfort initially and did the most soul-searching throughout grew the most.

Marie, a legal secretary from Cleveland, for example, told me how she struggled to take this opportunity for herself now that her third and youngest child left for college. She said that her schedule always had revolved around her kids' and her husband's agendas. Besides working, she had total responsibility for taking care of the house and cooking. She did try to go back to school once but dropped out because she felt overwhelmed with schoolwork in addition to all her other responsibilities.

Marie is confused about her obligations to others. "I feel like it's my turn now, but I don't know what it's my turn for. Is it my turn to be an individual? Is it my turn to do exactly what I have always wanted to do? Do I still have to take other people into consideration?" she queries. "They don't consider me. They don't ask me. They just say, 'Hey, I'm doing it.'" Marie struggles with the implications of putting herself first. She knows she could never disregard her family's feelings totally—nor would she want to. But like many women, she needs time to figure out how to find a balance so that she can respect others and still value herself.

STRIVING FOR BALANCE

Knowing what we do about women's development, it's clear that when we stop deferring to others, we don't become clones of the individuated male, exalted by male researchers such as Daniel

My Turn

Levinson. Rather, we strive to achieve more balance in our lives. As mothers, many of us pour our emotional energy into caring for and nurturing our families—including those of us who work outside the home. When our children leave, we are free to concentrate on ourselves and develop other interests and pursuits. Becoming more active, assertive, and aggressive complements our nurturing, caring qualities. Relationships still remain important to us, but *we* can set the parameters now.

Why do so many of us strive for balance at midlife? Have we been out of whack until now, in touch with only a part of our whole selves? David Gutmann, a psychologist at Northwestern University who has done extensive work on psychological changes at midlife, thinks so. He believes—with cross-cultural studies to support his contention—that the qualities called "masculine" and "feminine" are more tied to what he calls "the seasons of parenthood" than to biology. That is, during active parenting, our husbands (unconsciously) hand over the nurturing role to us, and we then express their softer, more passive side, while we turn over the aggressive role to our husbands, and they express our harsher qualities. When our children leave, these roles become unnecessary, Gutmann believes, so our husbands can express their more "feminine" sides, and we can become more "masculine." With the parental restraints lifted, we are both liberated to develop our entire potential.[19]

Many of the women I interviewed recognized that they and their husbands had stereotypical roles while raising their children and crossed over into each other's realm once their children left. For example, women told me that their husbands missed their children's presence now more than they did. The women felt relieved to give up their caregiving role and ready to move on with their own lives in the larger world. In contrast, their husbands, who played the more aggressive role as breadwinner for twenty-some years, wanted to ease up at work, spend more time with their families, and develop closer relationships with their children. This, just as the youngest child moved out. These men now realized that they had missed their children's growing up because they were working and wanted to make up for lost time, just as their children flew the coop.

In an interesting spin-off on Gutmann's theory, a landmark study of middle-aged urban American couples found that after the children leave, women become more dominant in the family and take on a more maternal and more managerial role toward their husbands. And here's the kicker: The husbands, rather than looking for new areas to master, become more self-indulgent and less responsible. In effect, they replace the child who left.[20]

Other theorists have written about how men and women strive to become whole at midlife, although they have not tied the earlier dichotomy to parenthood. Jungians, for example, believe that the "shadow," which represents everything that has been repressed or gone unrecognized, comes to the fore. This happens at midlife because people recognize their mortality and desire to live life more fully and honestly. When the "shadow" emerges, it helps bring the personality back into balance.[21] For women, this often involves a recognition and acceptance of their more masculine side, or animus. (For men it's the reverse: their anima, or feminine side, needs to be freed.)

Our children leaving home frees us from the constraints of caregiving and should allow us to express our "shadows," those untapped parts of ourselves. But because mothering has been such an integral part of our existence, many of us now feel uncertain and confused about our identity. A secretary said to me, "Who am I now? I am not just somebody's mother or somebody's wife. What have I accomplished? In my eyes, I guess, raising three children to be self-sufficient, but I have never done anything for just me. What *could* I get involved in? What do I really want? I don't know because I never had time to think about what I really want. I'm not really sure what makes me happy." A school principal echoed her words: "The primary force of my life was as a mother, and that's not there anymore. Who am I now?"

When our children leave, we must redefine ourselves. Of course, we are still mothers and always will be as long as our children live, but we are no longer actively mothering. We don't *feel* like mothers in the same way. Not only will our relationships with our children change in the coming years, but our identity will evolve, as will our feelings about ourselves.

Each of our experiences contributes to who we are today. Raising children changes us in countless ways. Who we are and who we become evolves *because* we have raised our children. We would be different people if we didn't have children and if we didn't have our particular children. Our mothering experiences, which are as diverse as we are, have a profound impact on our sense of self.

Every separation compels us to think about ourselves in a new way. The departure of our children—because they have been so central to our existence—becomes the catalyst for change. Letting them go emotionally sets us free. Enormous challenges lie ahead, as we stand on the brink of a new phase of our lives. Opportunities abound.

CHAPTER TWO

THE MOTHER BOND

What is your earliest memory of being a mother?

When I asked that question of Sarah, a 51-year-old psychologist with a private practice for twenty years, she recalled her daughter's birth: "I felt like I had truly witnessed the most extraordinary miracle that nobody ever had prepared me for or told me about. It was probably the single most significant event in my life. I felt in touch with God. I felt the goddess was this mountain inside of me just moving through.

"For about the first seven or eight months of her life, I felt I was in this endless miracle. I never let her out of my sight. I remember I couldn't take a shower 'cause I was terrified if I was taking a shower with the water running I couldn't hear her. I was enormously attached to her. I made every decision that was important around the framework of my being a mother. I went back to school because I knew I really needed to keep some contact with my mind. I couldn't just be a full-time mother. But I went back to school with an external degree program where you make your own program, so that I could schedule my own hours and be with her."

In answer to the same question, Dolores, age 58, who runs a business from her home, recalled how she felt when the nurse handed her her son in the hospital: "I looked at him and had this overwhelming sensation of love. As dearly as I love my husband, I never felt that. . . . I think being a mother is one of the greatest occupations on earth. No joke. I would argue about it with anybody. I can remember things that I didn't know were going to happen, like the 'mother-bear sensation.' I didn't know that this actually becomes a part of it, that protective instinct that rises to the surface. I remember very clearly when Dennis was little. The kid next door put my son's face down in the sand. Frankly I could have shaken that child's teeth out. What a terrifying thought—but he could have blinded Dennis or suffocated him."

Cynthia, 49, a public relations professional, answered this way: "I didn't feel what I thought you were supposed to feel. I didn't feel any of that bonding stuff in the hospital. My roommate was so happy, talking to this baby, and I swear, as the second of five kids, I'd had a lot of experience with babies, I felt comfortable with babies, but I just did not have that immediate we-are-in-this-together thing.

God, I was supposed to be so wrapped up in this kid, and I wasn't. I remember feeling extremely guilty about it."

Three different women, three different reactions to a common occurrence: the birth of their first child, the primal bonding experience. Sarah felt awed by the miracle of birth and connected immediately with her child. Although she organized her life around caring for her child, she also recognized that she needed something of her own, "some contact with my mind," as she put it. Dolores, on the other hand, shocked herself at the drastic measure she was ready to take to protect her child; in this, she recognized the depth of her attachment to her son. In contrast, Cynthia felt guilty before she and her son, Robert, even left the hospital, because she didn't feel that immediate connection, as she assumed all "good" mothers did.

The issues these three women expressed—attachment, separation, protection, and guilt—are part and parcel of the bond between a mother and her child. This complicated connection is influenced by personal, familial, political, and cultural forces. Only in understanding the depth and complexity of the bond can we appreciate fully the significance of our children's departure. When our children leave home, the bond—and all the intricacies that accompany it— shifts in innumerable ways, creating a domino effect on our lives.

CONNECTING

When exactly does a mother bond with her child? Is there a single moment, a click, when it happens? Or is it a gradual process? Ethological theorists, who study animal behavior, think a biological attraction may exist between a mother and her child that depends upon intimate contact immediately after birth. These theories assume then that if the mother and child are separated—

should the baby require a stay in an intensive care unit, for example—they cannot establish a bond, which, the theorists believe, may precipitate the mother rejecting the baby later.[1]

From my interviews and research, however, I've seen that many women do not connect immediately with their child at birth but do form a close link later. Some women, like Cynthia, take several months to bond emotionally with their child. One would expect this, because not all births are planned, wanted, or joyful. Not all women have the support of a caring husband, nor do they feel prepared emotionally for the demands of a newborn. Cynthia later told me her thoughts right before she went into labor: "I looked at Tim (her husband) and thought, we are so happy. How do you let somebody else—another life, another person—into this? I guess I expected him to be a person and he wasn't. He was just this little lump. I just did not know how to let a baby into my life." Even though Cynthia had planned her pregnancy and wanted her child, the day-to-day reality of caring for a baby differed greatly from her fantasy. The normal demands of the infant interfered with her idyllic relationship with her husband; the child became an intrusion, a lump.

Yet when she gave birth to a daughter two years later, Cynthia responded very differently. She remembers: "With Judith, I could not get my hands on her fast enough. I did feel really close to her immediately, and I think it was because I had the pleasure of knowing Robert. Oh boy, this is what it's about, this is what it's going to be like. I felt totally different about the second one." Cynthia felt she bonded instantly with her daughter, because she had gone through the experience with her son. She may have connected faster with a daughter for other reasons too. Perhaps having their shared gender created the immediate bond. Maybe some nebulous common tie—the shape of her daughter's nose, the look in her eye—reminded her of someone she cared about and made her connect instantly.

For Jane Lazarre, author of *The Mother Knot*, the "mother-feeling" didn't come until her son was almost 3 years old—something that tormented her for most of those years. She writes, "I sit on his bed and smooth his hair, pull the covers up, kiss him. Here it is, I think, sighing with relief. Here is the mother-feeling they talk about. It comes when your child is old enough to love you back, when you have known him for a while, when you are no longer physically suffering, when you have grown used to your life's changes, when you have no choice but to love him—more than a puppy you watched being born, more than a roomful of plants you shine fluorescent lights upon each evening, more than a long beautiful poem you have written over and over. . . . You love the child more. I had held my infant hour after anguished hour, worrying, Where are those feelings? And now here they are at last. . . . I am soothed. I walk back to the kitchen and touch his lunch box, all ready. . . ."[2]

Hundreds of such moments permeate our lives and reaffirm our link to and love for our children. Although birthdays and other celebrations mark important milestones, often the small, common moments can be most moving and most memorable, especially if you feel a special connection with your child. I remember one evening shortly after Andrew learned to read. An energetic, active 5-year-old, he never slowed down until he collapsed into bed. When I came into his bedroom to tuck him in, the room was dark except for a little reading light clipped to his headboard. Wearing his Superman pajamas, he was propped up on his pillow, eyes glued to his favorite book, *The Duck in the Truck*. A lump stuck in my throat as I leaned over to kiss him goodnight. I felt a swell of love and a common bond: yes, this is my son. He loves to read as I do.

THAT MOTHER-BEAR SENSATION

Women feel protective toward their children, just as animals do toward their young. Earlier in this chapter, Dolores called it "the mother-bear sensation"—that feeling that you'll do *anything* to protect your child. Maggie Singer, the mother of seven sons who was played by Susan Sarandon in the 1995 movie *Safe Passage*, knew that sensation viscerally. When her son, Percival, was knocked flat on the field while playing football, everyone in the stands rose to their feet, paralyzed, waiting for him to arise. Maggie waited for no one. She pushed everyone aside, raced across the field, picked him up, and carried him across the field to the locker room. When Percival came to, he was furious: "How *could* you?" he screams at her. "They have stretchers for things like that. You carried me like a baby and the guys saw? Why didn't you just leave me there?"

With tears streaming down her face, Maggie answers calmly, "I'm sorry, but I couldn't help it. When a woman becomes a mother, there's a little part of her that takes hold, and it just grows and grows. This monster-mother part, like the little thing in your cereal box that grows 300 times its original size. Well, when a woman becomes a mother, it rules her life, this monster-mother-300-times-bigger part. I saw you lying there. I wanted to help you. I couldn't see or hear anything else." She then tells Percival that he must quit football. He replies: "For today, you mean?" "No," she answers, "forever. It's too dangerous. I can't protect you."

Maggie Singer thinks she can protect her son, even though he is in high school. By the time most of our children are teenagers we realize, on some level, that we cannot keep them safe. A car can hit them within 30 feet of home; they can be abducted delivering newspapers in our neighborhood. But while they still live at home, we delude ourselves that we can protect them, that we assert some element of control. In fact, we usually can't, but because we see them everyday, can hold them and hug them, we retain the illusion that what happens to them is within our grasp.

Barbara Brownstein is a control freak, by her own admission. She has two daughters in their mid-twenties who have taken semesters abroad in such faraway places as Africa and South America. When they were younger, she worried about their riding in someone else's car without a seat belt. Today she worries about their flying in airplanes and biking in city traffic. An outwardly calm woman who speaks rapidly with an edge to her voice, she says, "It is not so much being apart from them that bothers me. It is worrying about what they are doing, where they are, and if they are safe. Issues of safety get me crazy." She bought her daughters a car with double air bags so they wouldn't have to bike in Chicago traffic. What she really wanted, she admits, was a Sherman tank. Then she'd feel that they were safe.

Now she worries less when they are away from home. "But when they come home, I get worse," she acknowledges. "I feel that old feeling—if they go out and take the car, I'm not able to go to sleep; I'm waiting to hear the car come up the driveway. They're in their twenties already! They drive all over the place. I wish I had the freedom not to worry where my kids are."

I know just what she means. Sometimes Margot drives from Seattle to San Francisco for a long weekend. When we discuss her plans on the phone, I'm concerned about who's going with her, whether they're driving at night, and who'll share the driving. But when I hang up, I go on with my business and put her plans out of my mind. When she's home, however, I often take on the responsibility and the worry, just like Barbara. The last time she came home, she went to visit a friend who lives in a marginal part of town. Before she left, I gave her a whole list of instructions: lock the car doors, don't get out of the car if anyone suspicious-looking is nearby, call if there's a problem. I thought that by giving Margot directives, I could keep her safe.

When our children physically leave the house and move to another part of town or another part of the world, the distance between us and them brings home the reality: We can no longer protect them. They are beyond our ken physically. The thought that our sons and daughters must navigate the world alone can be very frightening for us. But it can also bring us relief: We no longer have responsibility for them. They're on their own.

AMBIVALENCE REARS ITS HEAD

In the maternal bond, as in any love relationship, a dark side exists. Psychiatrist Eugene Bleuler first used the term "ambivalence" in 1911 to describe the coexistence of contradictory emotions—most commonly love and hate—toward the same person. He believed ambivalence was one of the fundamental signs of schizophrenia; today we consider ambivalence a universal emotion.[3] Yet until very recently, few women could admit that they had conflicting feelings about their child. Such an admission meant that they were bad mothers. When *The Mother Knot* was published in 1976, a *Washington Post* book reviewer lauded the author, Jane Lazarre, because she "ventured where no mother has ever ventured except under cover of fiction."[4] What did she write that created such a stir? Lazarre wrote honestly of her ambivalence—her fear, joy, helplessness, guilt, resentment, and love—about being a mother.

I remember resenting Andrew many times during his first few months but never breathing a word to anyone. My mother had done little to prepare me for motherhood, and since none of my friends had babies yet, I didn't feel comfortable talking to them. Dick and I planned this pregnancy; we wanted a child. My parents, who lived 700 miles away, eagerly awaited their first grandchild, and Dick's, who lived in town, looked forward to their fourth. But like Cynthia, I found the reality of caring for a baby very different from my fantasy. (I fantasized that I would be just like Jane Wyatt in *Father Knows Best*—always calm, patient, and understanding.) A 24-hour labor and rooming in (so I could nurse him around the clock) left me exhausted. When I got home from the hospital, I craved sleep, but Andrew wanted to eat every two hours. I'd rest between feedings—just close my eyes and doze off. Before I knew it, I'd hear his cry again. I'd cringe: Not again! I just fed you! But I roused myself, picked him up, shuffled over to the rocking chair, and nursed him. He sucked voraciously, his little fingers fumbling around my breast. It felt sweet to snuggle up with my baby and with the feeding over, I knew I'd get a brief respite.

Even though I was dead-tired, my pediatrician encouraged me to keep nursing on demand. Blindly, I followed his advice. I was locked into what Lazarre calls the "vicious lie"—the belief that "if a woman is *really* a woman, she will bear children graciously; if she is ultimately feminine, she will mysteriously know how to be a good mother."[5] When I didn't feel loving and eager to nurse every time I heard Andrew's cry, I assumed something must be wrong with me: I wasn't quite woman enough.

I adored my son, but I also resented how his presence had changed me from an energetic, take-charge person to a walking zombie. From that time on, I knew my life would no longer totally be my own. And herein lies the rub: loving my child and wanting to be there for him but needing breathing space to be me; wishing to be caring, loving, and nurturing *always* but only having so much to give.

Even today, the myth—that if you have "bad" feelings about your child, you are a bad mother—persists. When I asked my interviewees the open-ended question, "What was it like raising your kids?" the majority of women spoke in glowing terms about how much they enjoyed being a mother—despite many experiences to the contrary. For example, in answer to that question, one woman replied: "Having kids was the greatest thing. I thought if anybody ever finds out how wonderful this is, everybody will just want to have children. I loved having the children. I did all kinds of finger painting and went to feed the ducks. All of that." Yet later in our interview, she described how she agonized over problems her two kids had at school. Of course, many experiences seem better in retrospect than in actuality; we forget the agony of childbirth very quickly. But putting a uniformly positive cast on motherhood justifies all those years of service and makes us feel that, in the long run, the pain justifies the gain. Doing this, however, doesn't reflect a woman's total experience. Such denial does a disservice to mothers, particularly new ones, because they cannot be honest with their feelings and cannot receive the support they need. I know those early months after Andrew's birth would have been easier on me if I had been able to share my feelings with my mother or with close friends going through the same experience.

Fears of being devoured by motherhood usually surface most strongly during infancy, when we feel our child's utter dependence on us. Yet many of us struggle to balance our needs for attachment, belonging, and intimacy with our need for autonomy far beyond our child's infancy. Not all women feel this way nor at all times. But most of us must work to balance and mesh these often conflicting needs. A Philadelphia psychotherapist with three grown children described how she saw the conflict. She said, "The dilemma is once you say, 'Yes, I'm ready for my children to leave' and 'Yes, I have strong wishes for them to be independent,' at the bottom there is still this little core that feels empty. When I yearn to fill up that space that feels empty, what do I want? For me personally, it's to have all my children home, and then I remember what it really felt like, all the demands placed on me. And then I think how wonderful it is not to think about anybody but myself. That's the conflict."

The dilemma played out in her own family recently when her two daughters flew home from the West Coast for a family celebration. One afternoon, the three women happened to gather in the psychotherapist's bedroom. She stood at the ironing board, pressing her dress; one daughter was playing on the bed with her young son. The other daughter leaned against the wall, arms folded, looked around and said, "This scene makes me feel so safe." The psychotherapist laughed after she described the setting to me. "I know just want she meant," she said. "She meant let's just stay in this room for a few weeks!"

Balancing our desire to feel safe, secure, and close to people we care about with our need to venture out into the larger world troubles women in various ways at different times as their children grow up and after they leave home. Lois, a divorcee, told me she achieves balance by consciously compartmentalizing different parts of her self. We talked the day she expected her 20-year-old daughter home for winter break. "I've always been very cognizant of being three people," she explained. "I've been Lois, and I've been Sandie's mother, and I've been a professional counselor. And those three people, the priorities for those three people, are constantly getting juggled. Every day the priorities are different.

"Take what's happening tonight: She's coming home. So I'm kind of getting my professional stuff tied up so I can be her mother for the next couple of days. And when she's away, being her mother is a lower priority. When she's physically here, it's higher priority. When she's having a crisis (at school), it takes priority even though she's not here. Sometimes when I'm not taking care of myself, I'll say, 'Oh, my God, you haven't had your hair cut or your nails done. It's time for that.' . . . I was always very cognizant that sometimes I was first, and sometimes she was first, and sometimes my work was first. It's always been on the table with her too."

On the other hand, Mona, an outspoken single mother by choice, says she never had difficulty balancing conflicting needs, because her mothering was always peripheral to the rest of her life. She says, "I've always worked, and I've always thought my mothering was—this is going to sound very callous, and I don't mean it this way—tangential to who I was. Bonnie (her daughter) came into my life unexpectedly. I wasn't intending to get pregnant. We traveled our lives side by side, and I did what I needed to do for her. I'm not real dependent on her or dependent on being a mother as my defining role. . . . I want to make it clear that I adore this child, and we really have a wonderful relationship. And I'm grateful she happened into my life. That's how it feels to me."

Not many mothers speak with such detachment about their relationship with their daughters. *I'm grateful she happened into my life.* That sounds more like a phrase fathers would be apt to use. It indicates concern for and interest in the child but a certain distance as well.

FATHERS CONNECT DIFFERENTLY

Ask any woman and she'll tell you that her husband relates differently to their children than she does. Her husband can sleep soundly when their 17-year-old son has the family car out at 1 a.m., while she remains on red-eye alert. Her husband can pop in to a child's birthday party at the appointed hour, while she has spent days planning it. Experts have debated for years just why a father bonds differently than a mother with their child. Some believe that because a mother carries her child for nine months, it becomes a part of her, and she has a more visceral attachment. Many of us would vouch for this. Other theorists have suggested that mothers remain more responsive to their children because of innate biological, hormonal mechanisms.[6] Still others believe economic pressures and financial rewards keep men in the workforce and therefore less available to their children, while others argue that social conditioning perpetuates the male/female parenting differences.

In her highly acclaimed book *The Reproduction of Mothering*, sociologist Nancy Chodorow posits that women develop the mothering capacity and desire to mother because of the intimate bond they form with *their* mothers and their desire to recreate this. They do so by having their own children: Mothers form intimate ties with their daughters because of their shared gender. With their sons, whom they view as different, mothers encourage independence, not closeness. According to Chodorow, this separation process makes men more prepared for the world of work and public life and less involved in interpersonal relationships in the family.

Chodorow believes that the sexual and familial division of labor, in which women mother and are more involved than men in interpersonal relationships, produces a division of psychological capacities in their daughters and sons that leads women and men to repeat this pattern for generations.[7] Statistics bear this out: A 1992 study of 3,000 employed men and women found that only 5 percent of the men said they took major responsibility for child care *and housework*.[8] Child care is not synonymous with attachment or even caring, because parents can give a bath, check a spelling list, or read a story mechanically while thinking about a presentation for work. Still, participation in child care does measure parental involvement.

How do women feel about their husband's looser, more casual relationship with their children? In truth, some prefer it this way and collude to keep their husband at a distance. These women want things done their way, with everything under their control. They may subtly undermine their husband's authority by criticizing him for the way he disciplines a child, ignore his suggestions about a weekend outing, or initiate a family discussion when they know he's unavailable.

Many of us, however, feel angry and jealous of our husband's detachment and the ease with which he's able to have a life separate from fatherhood without experiencing as many conflicts as we. Author Lazarre recalls the morning when, in a fury, she tore up her own books then threw her husband's all over the apartment, ". . . hating him for still being involved in his work, for becoming a parent without having been pregnant or given birth, for holding the baby incorrectly and forgetting to put the dirty diapers out that morning, for making an appointment to go to a meeting when he knew perfectly well it was my day for the library, for suggesting each night as I lay down drowsily in front of the television that I study, for not offering to drive me to school so I could nurse before and after my class, for not being as fascinated with me as a mother as he had been with me as a writer or student, for being exhausted from studying and giving the 2 a.m. feeding, for not loving Benjamin as much as I did, and for having become a parent and still remaining—in the eyes of the world and himself—a person too."[9]

Many of us have felt such anger and resentment. It makes one wonder why we usually do bond more intensely than our husbands with our children. According to psychoanalytic thought, a primal, universal need exists, which usually remains unconscious, to recreate the bond with one's mother who is normally the primary caretaker and first emotional attachment for both females and males. A woman reconstructs the connection by raising a child; through mothering it, she becomes both mother and child at once. The man, in contrast, reproduces the maternal bond through a heterosexual relationship. The child, then, can become an intrusion[10] and, at times, a target of male jealousy.

In early marriage, most of us have an exclusive relationship with our husbands, in which they know they matter most to us. When our baby comes, this tiny creature usurps our husband's vaulted position. No matter how fascinating he is, we now have one ear attuned to our baby. My husband, who is more psychologically minded than most, admitted that he felt jealous when I nursed Andrew. He said he didn't like sharing me with another male. Rationally he knew I was feeding our son. Irrationally, he wanted all of me, all to himself: Andrew became the intrusion.

TWO WOMEN/ONE LIFE

While most men go off to work with hardly a backward glance at the homefront, women who work outside the home struggle and juggle to fit the two parts of their life into a unified whole. Work brings us satisfaction as a source of accomplishment and achievement. But work can become a source of anxiety and stress, creating additional demands on us and further ambivalence.

Erica Jong expressed the conflict between being a mother—like her mother and grandmother—and a writer in the following poem, written in 1979, which I tacked to my bulletin board many years ago:

Woman Enough

Because my grandmother's hours
were apple cakes baking,
& dust motes gathering,
& linens yellowing
& seams and hems
inevitably unraveling—
I almost never keep house—
though really I like houses
& wish I had a clean one.

Because my mother's minutes
were sucked into the roar
of the vacuum cleaner,
because she waltzed with the washer-dryer
& tore her hair waiting for repairmen—
I send out my laundry,
& live in a dusty house,
though I really *like* clean houses
as well as anyone.

I am woman enough
to love the kneading of bread
as much as the feel
of typewriter keys

under my fingers—
springy, springy.
& the smell of clean laundry
& simmering soup
are almost as dear to me
as the smell of paper and ink.

I wish there were not a choice;
I wish I could be two women.
I wish the days could be longer.
But they are short.
So I write while
The dust piles up.

I sit at my typewriter
remembering my grandmother
& all my mothers,
& the minutes they lost
loving houses better than themselves—
& the man I love cleans up the kitchen
grumbling only a little
because he knows
that after all these centuries
it is easier for him
than for me.[11]

Like Erica Jong, I wish I could have been two women: I'd love
to have baked challah every Friday, made homemade cookies, and
had a spotless house, but I needed, and still need, the intellectual
challenge of my work more. Yet I, too, was torn by my mother's
influence. A typical '50s homemaker, her life revolved around her

husband, her daughters, and her home. She strived for well-balanced meals, baked wonderful cakes, and in her spare time did volunteer work. One of my recurrent childhood memories focuses on her coming home from the local hospital in her cherry red smock, which matched her cherry red lipstick, after a day of waitressing in the hospital coffee shop or pushing the candy cart. When she wasn't volunteering at the hospital, she pored over the hospital auxiliary files at home, balancing their books. She also did stints as Brownie troop leader, Girl Scout cookie sale chair, and synagogue volunteer.

Not having a career, however, she never understood the importance of work to me. Yet she wanted copies of everything I wrote, and until the day she died, kept a folder of my articles, labeled "Patti's Writings," in the drawer next to the phone and showed anyone who asked what I had written lately. But she rarely asked *me* about my work in any depth; our conversations centered on recipes, clothes, furniture, and the kids. I didn't talk much about my work, because she seemed uncomfortable viewing me as a professional. In her presence, I was only a mother and a daughter; the professional writer became submerged.

When I interviewed accomplished professional women for my previous book, *Women, Mentors, and Success,* they told me that they didn't *feel* successful unless they were handling the homefront swimmingly too. Career achievement alone did not make them feel good about themselves; they needed to feel positive about the mothering piece as well to feel successful as women. They saw how work could undermine their self-esteem, particularly if they had high standards at the office and at home. In trying to do everything well, they set up an impossible task. Inevitably they would fall short of the perfection for which they strived and blamed themselves for not doing either job up to par. "I always feel guilty," an attorney told me.

"When I'm at work, I feel guilty that I'm not at home and when I'm at home, I feel like I should be working more."

As I write this chapter, Andrew, now 23, has moved back home to live with us for awhile. I feel some of the old conflicts and ambivalence resurfacing. When the children were teenagers, I rented office space in a nearby community to give me a separate space to write and distance from their friends, phone calls, and rock music. Last fall, with both children out of the house for two years, I decided to move my office back home. Little did I know that Andrew would end up living with us, his bedroom just 3 feet from my office. As I read my notes, going through transcripts of interviews, my mind veers off to a conversation I had with him last night, and my thoughts fly from my book. Or I am deep in thought, immersed in writing; yet part of me is pulled away, wondering what he's doing. I don't have conflicts anymore about concrete demands, like juggling carpools and cooking, but with Andrew home, at times I am dragged away emotionally from my work, my concentration broken, my thoughts splintered.

I interviewed a respected judge in her early sixties who told me that she thought women today get messages from the media that are just as powerful as the ones she received in the late 1950s and early 1960s that told women they were defective if they didn't enjoy staying home with their children and baking cookies. "The message the media sends women today is: Unless you have a big career, there is something defective about you," she said. "They are not saying you made the wrong choice but that there's something defective about you if you don't go to law school or medical school or get an M.B.A. I see women buying that message in the same way that I saw women thirty years ago buying the message that was beamed at me."

American culture idealizes motherhood, as increasing support for the family values campaign attests. We give mothers lip service by spending $225 million on Mother's Day cards,[12] yet society looks down on women who do not work outside the home and criticizes them for doing "nothing." Jill Johnson, a housewife and mother of two college-age sons who could afford to stay home to raise her children, felt this cultural condescension wherever she went. "I don't think there's any more important job than being a housewife and taking care of the kids," she says. "But we get very little credit for doing it. Quite frankly, it's a hell of a lot harder to be home with a bunch of kids than it is to be out in the workforce where you go and put in your time. Everybody's perfect, they're in their nice little suits, they've got their makeup on, everybody's happy, most of the time. You go home to where people are screaming, yelling they've had a bad day. Everybody's blaming you. You've got to get meals on the table. You've got to deal with everybody's emotional everything. I can remember when it was not cool to say you were a housewife. I thought that really stinks."

When her kids left home, she felt a loss of purpose. "What do I do now? Everything was geared toward family. I don't have all of the laundry, I don't have the regimen of having supper at a certain time. Those are perks to not having the kids around," she admits. "But the lack of purpose at first was really disheartening. For a woman who has spent most of her time geared toward children, it's like, 'Wow, what do I do now?' It was stressful." Jill went into counseling with an older female therapist. Using her as a positive role model, Jill started to concentrate on herself and to view this time as a true opportunity.

Whether or not we work outside the home, however, society blames us for our children's problems. If we stay at home, we are criticized for being overly involved in our children's lives, for loving them too much. If we work, we are faulted for not giving our children enough time and attention, for not loving them enough.

Because of our own guilt and self-blame—regardless of whether or not we work outside the home—we also buy into the cultural bias.

DOING IT ALL

How *do* we assimilate the cultural messages about working and mothering? Absorb the influence of our mothers and grandmothers? Cope with the reactions of our husbands, if we're married? And deal with our own personal anxieties? Maria deLuca often ponders these questions as she thinks about her own life. A 54-year-old math professor at a small college in the Midwest, she has two children finishing college. Maria grew up on a farm in California with her mother and four siblings. Her father walked out when Maria was 8 years old, leaving her mother to support the family. She worked in a packing warehouse and in the fields, yet every Sunday she baked two pies and a huge loaf of bread for the family's noontime meal. Maria started working on the farm when she was 9. "I had always had the feeling that maybe somehow I was not quite normal. You don't expect somebody growing up dirt poor to work toward an academic goal," she says, reflecting on her childhood. "I did not have the ordinary dreams and fantasies that most young women had about having a family. Actually having children deepened my concern of whether I could pull off normalcy. I had to look deep inside myself to see whether I could have a normal family."

I talked to Maria a year after Carlo, her husband of twenty-five years, also a college professor, ran off to Italy with one of his students. While Maria and Carlo were married, he expected a full breakfast and a complete dinner every night, continuing the tradition he grew up with. Maria became a gourmet cook. She also had full responsibility for their two kids, was finishing her dissertation, and taught a full load of classes. She explains, "Partly it was my husband requiring the meals, but it was also a family ritual and also something that I liked to do, and I could seemingly *do* it, so why not? We were all up at 7 a.m. for a full breakfast—scrambled eggs and hash browns or blueberry pancakes or whatever. Then, off to school, always late. I put on a totally different cap at the university. At 3:30 I went home, did nine yards of the mother things. Then, of course, the dinner meals. One night it might be teriyaki; the next night it might be beef stroganoff. Then helping the kids with their homework and interacting with them. At 9:00 I started on my own work. I would do that till midnight or 4 in the morning. Then I was up at 7 again." Her husband, while physically present every night, remained emotionally distant and uninvolved in the children's lives. Teaching and writing books demanded his attention.

Maria bought the message that she could have it all: the professional husband, the kids, the gourmet meals, and the high-powered career. With her mother as a role model, her husband pushing her to excel both as an academician and a gourmet cook, and her own insecurities about growing up poor, she had many gods to satisfy. Now with her husband on the other side of the world and her kids off at college, she is alone, exhausted, and sad. When Maria looks back on those years now, she says, *"Damn, how did I do that?"* Her voice quakes with emotion. "But then I looked around and I knew full well that all the women were doing it in their own ways. I did that for about ten years. I look back and I realize that I was very, very stupid."

A TRANSFORMING EXPERIENCE

When our children leave home and active parenting ends, we realize that the experience of being a mother and all that it entails has altered us irrevocably. When I asked the women I interviewed just how motherhood had changed them, their answers were as varied as the women themselves.

Sarah, a widow and the mother of a daughter living across the country, spoke softly and emotionally: "It made me very aware of the power of love and fragility of love. I really feel those two things go hand in hand. I don't ever take it for granted. I know it can be wiped out in a second, so it's very precious." She then draws my attention to a needlepoint on her kitchen wall that reads, "Children are the anchors that hold a mother to life." Sarah goes on, "If my daughter is the anchor that grounds me to life, then I feel like I want to be a good example to her. That's my part of the responsibility today: to really be a role model to her about how to live well."

When I asked that question of Sandy, a researcher and the mother of two sons, she drew on her childhood experiences: "Motherhood taught me what it means to compromise and how to be creative in meeting my needs when I was third on the list—after my husband and the kids. I don't think I was a spoiled child, but my sister was sick when we were growing up, so my mother kind of revolved around her. I got everything that I needed—I wasn't neglected—but I wasn't first on the list. That's been my metaphor. When I say I'm getting my life back now, I mean I'm putting myself first on my list." Sandy has no regrets today about being third on the list for so long, because her kids have turned out to be "really nice people." She says, "I think that's a payoff for being first on somebody's list."

MY TURN

Mona, a teacher and single parent, was one of the few who spoke negatively about the experience: "I felt like motherhood derailed me. Not that I know what track exactly I was on before, but I feel like it made a forty-five-degree-angle turn in my life. I would describe myself as something of a free spirit before Bonnie [her daughter] was born. When you have to provide a home and have a stable place for schooling and all that. . . ." Her voice trails off. With Bonnie's leaving, Mona says, "I want to get back to my youth or to a certain freedom I never felt I had being responsible for a child."

Molly, a chemist and the mother of two children who chose nontraditional paths, learned far more than she ever anticipated: "My kids taught me a whole lot. I had very much a one-way view of the world—one way of doing things, one path to take. My daughters have done things differently from me, and the times have changed also." Because of her parenting experiences, she says, "I've been able to look at the world in a broader, more diverse way than the way I originally envisioned things."

These four women articulated some of the ways motherhood altered them, but many others found its transforming nature difficult to put into words, so basic and profound were the changes. If a woman is intensely involved in caring for her children, motherhood will affect her at the deepest level of her personality. In her book *Stories from the Motherline*, psychologist Naomi Ruth Lowinsky eloquently described the metamorphosis she experienced: "The physical experience of giving birth changed my universe. . . . Before that birth I was quite another person. I had been an intellectual maiden curled up in a chair reading T. S. Eliot and asking Prufrock's question: 'Do I dare/Disturb the universe?' Could I write great poetry? Could I be original? The everyday miracle of birth changed my orientation in life. Like every other mother in the world, I had dared to pass through the dark gate; I had dared to bear new life. . . .

An intellectual maiden died and a woman, his mother, was emerging into life. I knew in my body the sacred connection of all human life to the female body. I had not disturbed the universe. The universe had moved through me. I was part of everything that was alive. I had carnal knowledge of my own female nature. It would take me a full generation to find words to express what I knew then.

"I felt at once whole and broken, fulfilled and empty, vibrant with life and sorely wounded. My mother visited me and her quiet presence grounded me and soothed me."[13]

Motherhood forces us to grow up. Psychoanalyst Therese Benedek, who has written extensively on parenthood as an adult developmental phase, notes: "Women have a better chance to achieve completion of their physical and emotional maturation through motherhood than they have if motherhood is denied to them."[14] Our children raise us as much as we raise them; they influence us just as we influence them. Through the experience of mothering, we come to know ourselves in a different way. Our sense of self evolves as it expands to include our identity as a mother.[15] The nature of our mothering experience determines just how it affects our own identity.

Each of our experiences depends on many factors, including the issues each of us brings as a woman and a daughter, the fit between us and each of our children, the degree of support we have, and the amount of ambivalence we harbor toward the experience. In an interesting study, British psychoanalyst and research psychologist Joan Raphael-Leff identified two distinct approaches to motherhood that determine how profoundly it affects a woman. Women in the first group, whom she calls Facilitators, see motherhood as a much-desired state of self-realization, expect it to be rewarding, and adapt themselves to their child's needs. They feel comfortable with the child's dependence; going to work can be problematic and conflictual for this group of women.[16]

Facilitators see motherhood as part of their core self, so the experience affects them more profoundly than it does other women. Consequently, the child's departure is more traumatic for them. Many of the women I interviewed fit this category. Like me, they married in the mid-1960s to early 1970s with the expectation that their fulfillment would come through motherhood. But many of us had experiences that did not meet the cultural ideal we saw on *Ozzie and Harriet* or *Father Knows Best*. Most of us started working while our children still lived home and now have full-time jobs or full-fledged careers. But those old tapes—those programmed messages gleaned from our mothers and grandmothers—still play in our heads. Even as I sit here, writing my fourth book with seventeen years as a writer under my belt—only six years less than my tenure as a mother—I know that no career setback even touches how I feel when something troubling happens to one of my children.

The second group of women, who Raphael-Leff calls Regulators, perceives motherhood as a role to be assumed and relinquished, not an essential part of their core self. These women train their child to fit into *their* routine and look forward to returning to their former lives. The child's needs feel overwhelming to these women, so they are more likely to turn to someone else, such as a spouse, mother, or day-care provider, to perform the daily care. Work represents freedom and does not pose as many conflicts.[17]

These women will not feel the same depth of emotion in motherhood; when their children leave home, they cast aside the mothering role. Mona, who said earlier that motherhood derailed her, fits this category. She put in her time with her child, albeit in a thoughtful and earnest way, but now wants to return to her former life. She spoke of motherhood as an interesting experience, almost as one would describe a vacation or gourmet meal. She donned motherhood like a hat for eighteen years, not a life-defining experience. When her daughter went to college, she says, "For about a week I was really at a loss, in the house wandering around, really missing her. After that point, I have not had very many periods of wanting to be with her." Mona enrolled in a graduate program and went on with her life. She did not experience the soul-searching or identity confusion that many women in the former group experienced because motherhood was a role, not a major part of her identity.

Raphael-Leff's categories are helpful as a way of conceptualizing women's orientation to motherhood. But her framework is too simplistic for the way most of us feel about being mothers and about working. Of course, it's difficult to quantify feelings and emotions, but by labeling two extremes, she has not accounted for the nuances and ambivalences we all feel. For many of us, work is crucial *and* so is motherhood. We feel invested in both and gain parts of our identity from both. Sometimes work matters more and at other times—if we have a sick or hurt child—we only care about our families.

The complexity of our allegiances and ambivalences was reinforced when I talked with an attorney who practiced for seven years before she got pregnant. She took off four months after the birth of each of her two children, then resumed her 70-hour work week. She told me: "Being a mother is not my primary identity. I think of myself as a professional first." And yet she added, "But my family is my highest priority, and I won't sacrifice anything to do with my children." Hearing her conflicting comments confused me: How can she say that her primary identity is as a professional, and yet her family is her highest priority? Judging from the hours she spends at the office and the passion with which she approaches her work, I do believe that she thinks of herself as a professional first. But she probably feels guilty about the long hours she spends at the firm and worries about neglecting her family. Giving herself the message that her family is her highest priority enables her to work guilt-free. She rationalizes her long hours by saying to herself, "What I'm doing is OK because I really care about my family." She has made an unconscious compromise, which allows her to work and feel all right about it. We all make such trade-offs and rationalizations to justify our choices.

Whether or not we see motherhood as part of our core identity, however, few of us escape unchanged. Like every significant relationship, motherhood has touched us and transformed us in some way, adding another layer to our understanding of ourselves. We may not like everything we learned, but we found our mettle.

Certainly motherhood has matured us: We've grown smarter and wiser. Motherhood has tested us, unlike any other relationship. Unquestionably, motherhood has empowered us. We've garnered our strength for years. Now the time has come to invest our energy in ourselves. First, we must put our role in perspective as one factor in our children's development. Then, liberated and whole, we will feel ready to move on.

CHAPTER THREE

WHERE DID I GO WRONG?

My father, an immigrant with an eighth grade education, came to America in search of opportunity. He left Lithuania in 1925 at age 25 and settled in Wisconsin where his uncle owned a furniture store. My father drove the delivery truck by day and at night went to school to learn English. When he died in 1979, he was vice president of the company—not that he cared about the title. He worked ten-hour days six days a week, he told us, so he could afford to send my sister and me to college. "Get a good education," we heard hundreds of times growing up. "No one can take that away from you." He often joked that he went to the School of Hard Knocks, but his daughters would not. Any expense for school or books was never questioned. He greeted all other requests for money with: "Do you really need this?"

My father didn't have difficulty convincing me of the value of an education. I loved school, always had my nose in a book, and made straight A's in high school. I think I became a writer in part so I could be a perennial student. I could get paid for doing what I loved: reading, writing, studying, and discussing ideas. With each new project, I could learn and challenge myself.

I tried to impart my love of learning and books to our kids, though I never preached as blatantly as my father did. Still, they got the message. Our weekly trips to the library began before they could read. I always had a stack of books at home, usually reading two at a time. They often saw me curled up with a good novel or heard me shushing them to hold on until I finished just one more page. My husband, Dick, shared my values but for different reasons. He felt *he* didn't get a good education. Although he went to a prestigious college, he just "got by" without studying or learning much and, in retrospect, felt he missed an important opportunity. Both our children, Andrew and Margot, enjoyed reading and school through the elementary grades, but by middle school, Margot was more interested in boys, and Andrew had gravitated to a tough crowd. Learning was no longer "cool" and school became a place to socialize.

Dick and I offered them the option of going to a private high school, hoping that small classes and more individual attention would turn them on to learning. Surprisingly, both wanted to transfer. The Quaker school suited Margot well; she enjoyed learning by discussion rather than memorization and doing projects and papers for finals instead of quizzes. By her senior year she was thriving in a competitive, academic environment. Nevertheless, her passion remained the Grateful Dead, and she attended as many concerts as she could when the band played on the East Coast.

Andrew continued getting B's without working much, always doing just enough to get by. He was accepted by the college of his choice, but a month before he was set to leave, he decided he wasn't ready and deferred for a year. When he went to a large university the following September, he seemed more mature and ready for the college challenge.

At the end of his freshman year, however, Andrew told us he didn't want to go back to school. He wasn't sure what he wanted to do in the fall. He felt unmotivated and purposeless. We talked and talked. At our urging, he went to the university counseling service but stopped after a couple of sessions. In August he told us he found a technical school where he could study music technology, his major in college. He'd get more hands-on experience with less theory, he argued, and they'd place him in a job after two years. We consented, rationalizing that at least he would be in *some kind* of school. But by November he had dropped out.

I felt disappointed and embarrassed. All our friends' kids were in college. *Everyone* went to college today. I was filled with guilt and convinced that his dropping out was my fault. I pushed education too hard. I didn't teach him how to persevere when things get tough. I should've, would've, could've. . . . I had a million reasons to explain why I had caused this problem. At bottom, I was convinced that I was a lousy parent. Good parents have good kids, kids they are proud of, kids who follow the traditional path.

Margot began her freshman year the same September that Andrew started the technical school. In mid-December, however, she called home to tell us that *she* wanted to "take some time off" to follow the Grateful Dead. Again, we talked and talked but to no avail. Now I felt a double stigma: I had not just one but two children who had rejected me and my values. I could no longer look to Margot and feel, I must have done *something* right, at least she's in school. Now I felt twice branded as a terrible mother.

This double whammy—only a semester after Margot left for college—came at a time when I had expected to feel a sense of accomplishment for having successfully launched my children into the adult world. Instead, like many of the women I interviewed who were disappointed in their children, I struggled to put my mothering experience in perspective now that the kids had left home. Just when I thought that my involvement in active parenting would end, I was drawn in deeper. How could I let go when I felt that my job wasn't done, or certainly not done right? I knew exactly what psychologist Lillian Rubin meant when she wrote that for the woman who is disappointed with her child, separation is more difficult, because "she's stuck with feelings of incompletion—with the sense that one of life's tasks is not finished, yet is now outside her control."[1]

Neither of the children lived with us immediately after they dropped out of school, but my thoughts and emotions were tied up with them constantly. I dwelt on the past: How did this happen? What caused it? Where did we go wrong? I worried about the future: Would they ever go back to school? What if they really got off track now? I tried to stay in the present and just live my life, but I couldn't let go—yet.

A TIME OF REFLECTION

Our children's departure is a milestone, a natural demarcation, a time to reflect and reassess: How'd I do? Most parents, and most of society, judge how they did by looking at the result—how their children turned out. In their twenties, our children are not yet finished products; they will continue to evolve and grow. But with active parenting over, we feel we've made our major contribution. Nonetheless, most of us have regrets. Of the forty-five women I interviewed, almost every one told me she regretted *something* about her parenting. Women told me they'd wished they had been stricter, that they'd had more fun with their children, that they'd had more money to spend on extras, or that they'd held their child back a grade.

Of course, we mothers alone are not responsible for how our children turn out. But because of the intensive mother-blaming in our society, we usually take the rap when our children don't follow the traditional path or suffer with emotional problems. Yet many other factors influence our children: their temperament and personality, their peers, their siblings, their fathers, and the culture around them. In this chapter, I'll explore these influences to help us put in perspective our role and impact as one factor—not the *only* cause—in the way our children develop.

Generally we feel good if our child is heterosexual, not doing drugs, in college, and functioning reasonably well. We have a sense of accomplishment and pride. We feel comfortable launching our child into the larger world. When we can say, "There's a job well done," that sense of accomplishment transcends any feelings of loss; the relief is unequivocal.[2]

That's exactly how Dana Kramer felt. A 54-year-old teacher who has been both widowed and divorced, she owns a strong sense of accomplishment. She has three sons in their twenties. One is still in college; the other two practice law. "I feel good about my kids," she says. "I feel like I personally did as good a job as I could have done under my particular set of circumstances. I think my three young men have grown up to be really very decent, kind young men. I say that now because over the years, I've had teachers of theirs and parents of friends of theirs say to me, 'Dana, you've really done a great job.' I used to be embarrassed and say, 'Oh, no, it wasn't just me.' Not long ago I got to the point where I just say 'Thank you.' You know what? It *was* me."

Women who are disappointed in how their children turned out feel relieved too, but their consolation comes from knowing that they no longer have to confront issues and problems every day. Relief for them is mixed with painful feelings of failure.[3] In my interviews, many, many women expressed dissatisfaction with their children, their children's lifestyles, or their children's choices. These women struggle—some to this day—to come to terms with their feelings of failure and to understand their part in how their child developed. They bear out what Lillian Rubin found almost twenty years ago: "It's impossible for a mother to experience disappointment in her children without blaming herself."[4]

WHOSE LIFE IS IT, ANYWAY?

Most of us would deny that we see our children as extensions of ourselves, yet many of us get into trouble for that very reason: We put *our* expectations on our children and then feel disappointed when *they* don't fulfill our goals and dreams. Of course, we know intellectually that our children are separate individuals, but emotionally we want them to behave in a certain way—our way. Remember when our toddlers screamed at the top of their lungs at the supermarket because *they* wanted to decide which cereal went into our shopping carts? Those outbursts were our kids' way of saying "I'm different," "I'm going to do what I want—not what you want me to do." Even then, they got the best of us. They embarrassed us in public. Now our kids are young adults. Certainly, we know they have minds of their own and lives of their choosing. They no longer live at home, so we really don't know what they do with their friends, where they go, or even how they live. Yet we still want them to do what we want, to behave more like us, to fulfill our expectations. Why? Is it that we don't trust them? That we want to control them? That *we* know what's best for them?

We want our sons and daughters to make us look good to the outside world—to be attractive, accomplished, and mentally healthy. How easy to feel disappointed, then, when a child doesn't live up to *our* aspirations. Rosalie Stern felt so embarrassed and ashamed when her single daughter got pregnant and decided to keep her child that she didn't tell any of her friends until the baby was born. For nine months, Rosalie lived in silence with her secret, often blaming herself for her daughter's behavior. Imagine the burden Rosalie carried: censoring her words, watching that she didn't slip, yet wanting desperately to unburden herself. After the baby came, she began cautiously telling a few close friends whose children also had problems, because she knew they'd be accepting. Gradually, she told a widening circle of friends, family members, and acquaintances. Much to her surprise and relief, no one blamed her.

Women also told me of similar disappointments when their children married someone of a different religion, race, or background, and of their struggle to accept their child's homosexuality. Anne Dorfman, a petite, athletic woman who runs a nonprofit organization, had a very difficult time accepting that her daughter, Melissa, was a lesbian. She came out to her parents when she was in her third year of college. Anne told me, "I felt guilty, ashamed, that it was my fault. It was my husband's fault. It was our fault. I did not want to tell anybody at the time. I looked back to her childhood and said, 'Well, she cried too much,' 'I picked her up too much,' 'I didn't pick her up enough.' The first couple of months were just awful. She gave us some books to read, and she told us about an organization for parents that I became very involved in. Then I began telling my friends, and they didn't think that I was such a terrible mother. They didn't think it was my fault.

"Never for a moment did I think that I wasn't going to love her, support her, or care about her. None of that. Just a terrible disappointment that the hopes and dreams and expectations you want for your child. . . ." Her voice trails off as a sadness creeps in. *The hopes and dreams and expectations you want for your child.* That phrase says it all: The hopes, dreams, and expectations belong to us as parents. Our children may—and often do—have very different visions and plans for their lives. Anne says she envisioned her daughter with "a lovely career that would be very much part of her life, but she would also get married, have children, and have a white picket fence to boot." This was not her daughter's vision.

When our children have difficulty adjusting to mainstream society, we ache—for them and for us. We are shocked, sickened, saddened. Part of us wants to rush in and comfort them: "It's all right, baby, everything will be OK." Another part of us feels repulsed. We want to distance ourselves from them: "How *could* he?" we say. "Where did he come from? Where are the values I taught him?" Another part of us mourns their lost potential: "She is so bright. She could have done anything. How did she end up like this?" These were the laments I heard from a woman whose daughter walked out on her 3-year-old child and husband, from a woman whose son, "the golden boy," drinks too much and drives too fast, and from a woman whose son is in jail for murder.

Were these women's expectations too high? They would probably say that they didn't have unusually lofty standards for their children: They simply wanted them to be responsible, healthy, and law-abiding. Is that asking so much? For these children, yes. They have emotional problems, which their parents may have denied or minimized in their zeal to mold their sons and daughters to fit their parental expectations. The "acting out" behavior of these young adults is evidence of their deep, internal struggles.

Our own problems may seem trivial compared to the ones just described, and by most standards, they are. What do I, with two children who dropped out of college, have in common with someone whose daughter walked out on her family? We all share feelings of loss, disappointment, shame, guilt, and responsibility, but certainly the intensity and pervasiveness of our feelings differ depending on the woman and the situation. Still, the *process* is the same: We all must learn to accept our child for who he or she is.

Sharon Mintz, the woman whose son committed a murder, struggled long and hard with acceptance. When she learned that her son, Tim, had strangled a man, she was devastated and enraged: "How could my son do something like this? I didn't raise him to be like this." For six months, she refused to have anything to do with him. During that time she learned that he was schizophrenic. The diagnosis brought her some relief, because it offered an explanation for his behavior. Gradually she came to realize, "I can't abandon my son, no matter what he did. I don't approve of what he did, I don't condone it, but I can't abandon him. He's my son.

"The way he turned out is a great disappointment," Sharon says. "But if Tim had diabetes or heart trouble, it's the same. Once the initial shock is over, it's the same feeling. He's your child. I'm not proud of what he did, but I do love him."

How has Sharon finally come to accept her son? "I do a lot of talking to myself, meditation. Just dipping deep, deep, deep inside of me. It's a leap of faith," she says. "It's turning yourself over to whatever power is within and just trusting it. When I became well enough to be able to let go and say, 'Okay, I need help,' it worked. That's when I got the strength."

Sharon found strength by having faith in her higher power. Each of us needs to find our own way to accept our children as they are, as separate individuals. No easy task, this. First, we have to let go. Letting go means letting them be, not trying to change them, not trying to squeeze them into our mold of how a son or daughter should be. It means just letting them exist as they are—warts and all. It means accepting that they're not perfect and realizing that they have probably not turned into the ideal young adults we fantasized about when we snuggled them in our arms as newborns. They are who they are, and that's all right.

If we can change some of our attitudes, we will have an easier time accepting our children. Look for the positives in your situation, and seek your child's strengths. You may have to search hard and long. They may not be what you hoped for, but they are there. Instead of dwelling on the fact that your son is in a God-awful rock band, remind yourself that he has musical talents and this is his way of expressing them—for now. Rather than lamenting that your daughter will not follow your footsteps and become an attorney, focus on what she *can* do within the parameters of her own abilities.

As you emphasize the positives, try to let go of more of the negatives. Before you start obsessing about the negatives, ask yourself: How important is it? We mothers tend to get caught up in details, a lot of negative details. Does it really matter that he didn't call his sister on her birthday? Or that her room looks like a cyclone tore through it every time she comes home? Let the little things go, and keep the big picture in mind.

When we allow our children to lead their own lives, they will learn by natural consequences. Without our expectations and controls, they will be free to fail and succeed by their own actions. Rather than lecturing them on what's best for them or on what they really *should* do (remember how we hated it when our parents did that?), step back and allow them to find their own way. Only then will they internalize what they have learned. And we will be set free.

UNFINISHED BUSINESS

Jung once observed that the largest burden a child must bear is the unlived life of the parents.[5] When we have regrets about what we did or did not do in our past, we may unknowingly pass on our unfinished business to our children. Most of the time we do this unconsciously and have no idea how our actions and words affect our children—until the damage is done. In doing this, we also set up our children for failure, because we have not recognized their abilities, strengths, and limitations as being different from our own.

Elizabeth Green, a public affairs officer of a West Coast university, learned this the hard way. Only in hindsight did she see how her own educational deficit played out in her relationship with her son. Her parents sent her to a junior college so they could afford to finance a four-year college education for her two brothers. Neither of the brothers graduated. Elizabeth married after finishing the junior college and worked to put her husband through graduate school. For years, she felt embarrassed that she did not have a college degree, particularly since she worked in an academic setting and had so many professional friends. When her kids entered high school, she went back to school at night and finally garnered the sheepskin, what she called "the platinum key," several years ago.

But Elizabeth was determined that her son, Keith, a hale-fellow-well-met who was never a good student, would not suffer the shame she had endured. "I had a lot invested in his doing better than he did. Tremendous, tremendous expectations, so that at almost any time he knew full well that he was disappointing me," she said. "Of course, I didn't know this at the time, or I would have changed my behavior. I used to monitor everything he did. I always worked every conversation around to basically, 'Have you written your papers?' and 'Did you do your homework?'" At 11 p.m. the night before his college graduation, with dinner reservations waiting at the finest restaurant in town, Keith told his parents he didn't have enough credits to graduate. "It was shocking," says Elizabeth, "to think of the kind of lie he had to live."

Elizabeth felt betrayed by her son. Until the last moment, she believed he had completed the requirements for graduation. In retrospect, however, she says that in her heart of hearts, she knew he would not graduate. "I am in the education game, and I know when you are not performing. But I also know that they kick you out if you get lower than a two point," she says, trying to make sense of what she knew. "I know all that stuff but Keith is extremely handsome and totally charming and he has always gotten by on that." Today Elizabeth recognizes that she set herself up for disappointment. She knew that Keith wasn't "a student" and yet in her zeal to ensure that he not suffer the same humiliation she had, she ignored his abilities and pressured him to achieve.

In the aftermath of Keith's announcement that he could not graduate, Keith, Elizabeth, and her husband, Brad, entered family therapy. They worked together in understanding what had happened. Keith insisted that he *did* want to finish school, so with their therapist's help, they set ground rules: He could move home for a year while he finished school, provided he stayed in therapy. If he did not graduate at the end of the year, he had to move out.

During that year Elizabeth worked hard at pulling back and stopped "taking Keith's temperature." Each month, Elizabeth and Brad reminded Keith that he would need to move out in May if he had not completed his courses. Come May, they read their son the riot act—a traumatic experience for all three. Four days later, Keith had moved all his belongings into a friend's apartment with these angry parting words: "You are not going to have my love. I am not going to be in your life."

At first Elizabeth was crushed at Keith's response. But she did not waver, thanks to the support of her husband and therapist and her belief that she had done the right thing. In the last two years, the Greens have worked hard to rebuild their relationship with Keith. He has still not finished college. But Elizabeth has resigned herself to the facts: "I still wish he'd graduate," she says. "But I can't make him do it."

If Elizabeth's actions and reactions remind you of your own, take time to consider the repercussions for yourself and your family. Trying to control a young adult can lead to rebellion and conflicts: How can he follow his own heart when he has to satisfy you? Not only can this situation program your child for failure, but it can cause him to doubt himself and lose confidence.

Try to put your focus back on your own life. What can you do now to "finish" your own unresolved issues? Carefully explore all your options. If it's truly too late to make changes in a particular area, then try to let it go. We all have regrets at this stage of our lives; they are part of living.

BLAME THE MOTHER

In her book, *The Myth of the Bad Mother*, Jane Swigart, Ph.D., a mother and a therapist, explores how our society has created the twin myths of the Bad Mother, who is responsible for her children's emotional problems and unhappiness, and the Good Mother, who is selflessly devoted to her children's well-being.[6] In a nutshell, she says that our society has divided mothers into two groups: good ones who make their children happy and bad ones who make their children miserable. In reality, of course, all mothers are both good and bad to varying degrees. As we saw in the last chapter, most of us feel ambivalent toward our children; we feel both love and rage. Society has given women almost the entire responsibility for nurturing our children, and yet it blames us, as Bad Mothers, when such nurturance falls short of perfection.[7] It's our fault if our children are unhappy or have emotional problems.

Working mothers feel an added burden. Many of us feel conflicted about working and mothering under so-called normal conditions; when one of our children has problems, we feel an additional responsibility. Then society adds to our guilt by blaming us for not "being there" for our children.

Mental health professionals have done little to set the record straight. From the beginning of the twentieth century until the present day, they have perpetuated the myth of the Bad Mother in their practices and their writings. Psychoanalytic understandings of childhood disturbances have tended to blame the mother, rather than help her understand her relationship with her child.[8] Beginning with psychoanalyst Frieda Fromm-Reichmann's coining of the term "schizophrenogenic mother" (a mother who causes schizophrenia) in 1948, much of psychopathology, from juvenile delinquency to simple behavior problems, has been attributed to the mother.[9] In finding a scapegoat and a single cause, these theories overlook the complex basis for most psychological problems.

One theorist, Donald Winnicott, a pediatrician turned psychoanalyst, seemed aware of the damaging nature of mother-blaming and the guilt it provoked in women. He attempted to emphasize the positive nature of mothering by stressing the need for women to be "good enough"—not perfect—for their children to thrive and develop healthfully.[10] But even the expectation that mothers be "good enough" still puts the onus on us.

With the advent of the women's movement, one would have hoped that mother-blaming would cease. Unfortunately, it has not, according to a study of its occurrence in 125 major psychology and psychiatry clinical journals. Two Canadian researchers found that journal authors blamed mothers five times more than fathers for specific problem behavior. None of the articles described the mother or her relationship with her child as simply healthy, nor did the authors ever portray her only in positive terms. For instance, in one family, the author described the father as a 35-year-old bricklayer who was "healthy"; the mother, simply "nervous." The researchers also found that female clinicians were just as likely as male clinicians to blame mothers for their children's problems.[11]

This study has disturbing implications. First, the myth of the Bad Mother is alive and well in the 1990s, despite the women's movement and our more advanced understanding of the complex nature of emotional problems. In many instances, when women are aware of problems with their children and seek counseling, they run the risk of being blamed—rather than supported—by male *and* female therapists. This harms both women and their children, because neither can get the help they need. It's disheartening, too, that the very people we revere as experts are also vulnerable to society's prejudices.

We women also perpetuate the myth of the Bad Mother. Competition begins as soon as we become mothers. Remember how we used to query each other: When did your daughter walk? Start solids? Say her first words? We made mental notes of whose child did what when, as though their progress reflected their mothering. We looked critically at women whose children threw temper tantrums in public: Can't *she* control him? When our kids got older, the honor roll student, the student council president, and the star Little League player become trophies for us, outward signs of a job well done. Many of our cars sported bumper stickers reading "My child is a Bala Cynwyd Middle School honor student," or still bear window decals from Harvard and Yale. I've been to many parties in which the conversation focuses on what the children are doing (read "achieving"), not on the parents' lives.

Rivalry among parents affects fathers too, as Margot observed when she came home for spring break last year. I took her to a physician, the father of two college-aged sons attending prestigious universities, for a minor problem. His first question to her was, "Where are you going to school?" Afterwards she said to me, "What difference does it matter *where* I go to college? Why couldn't he just ask me if I was happy?"

Obviously, fathers are not immune to competitiveness. But most men do not have the same stake in parenting that women do, nor do they face societal blame when their children develop emotional problems or choose a nontraditional path. As evidence of this, we might consider such films as *The Graduate* and books such as *Catcher in the Rye* and *Portnoy's Complaint*. They exaggerate their portrayal of insensitive, overbearing mothers—not fathers.[12]

INDIVIDUAL DIFFERENCES

Although we mothers are easy targets for blame, many other factors influence our children's development. Differences in temperaments can have far-reaching effects. Years ago, experts thought babies were blank slates, tabulae rasae, to be written on by their environment. Now we know that newborns come into the world with their own personality and temperament. Studies have shown that even during the first 48 hours of life, babies respond differently to sounds, visual stimuli, and pacifiers. Infants also show differences in their ability to be soothed. Some of these measures of temperament remain constant a year later.[13]

Just how our child's temperament and personality mesh with our own determines the "fit": how we tune in to each other and respond emotionally.[14] When the "fit" is bad, it doesn't mean that the fault lies with either us or our baby but simply that our personalities or temperaments clash. A very calm, quiet mother, for example, may have difficulty with a hyperactive baby. She may constantly try to quiet and control him to match her more placid ideal of the "good" child. This mother may feel frustrated because the baby won't or can't conform. On the other hand, a mother who thrives on noise and activity may see a highly active baby as an affirmation of her style and enjoy his personality. They reinforce each other, and both feel good. Imagine the cumulative effect of these two pairings as the children grow up.

Just how different styles of parenting interact with various temperaments was the focus of one of the best-known studies on temperament—the New York Longitudinal Study. Child psychiatrists Stella Chess and A. Thomas sampled 133 children of New York middle-class professionals and followed them from infancy to adulthood. They found that some difficult children became difficult adults, but not all. When some of these children experienced a good "fit" with their parents or faced few or no stressful life events, they did well as adults. Chess and Thomas concluded that the strongest factor in predicting adult behavior is the temperament of the child, *not the quality of mothering.*[15]

My Turn

In addition to differences in temperament, some children are more resilient than others. We all know people who have an ability to muster a positive, optimistic outlook—no matter what happens—and to mobilize their own resources to cope.[16] Resilience seems to be determined by temperament and affected by the family environment. Resilience helps explain why one brother raised in poverty by a single, abusive parent becomes a physician and the other becomes a drug addict. It helps us understand, too, why some children raised in comfortable suburban homes with two loving parents are unable to function in mainstream society, while others become productive citizens. The difference in how these children turn out may have less to do with their mothering and more to do with their individual differences, particularly their resilience.

Understanding individual differences can remove the onus from us mothers. How can everything be our fault if our children came into the world with their own temperament, emotionality, personality, and degree of resilience? We cannot control these factors. Think about how these individual differences play out in your own family. Consider how each of your children differed from one another while they were growing up: How did each handle new situations? Separations? Challenges? Look at them today. Recognizing firsthand the differences within your own family may help release you from taking all the blame for the way a particular child has developed.

THE IMPACT OF OTHERS

We are all part of a community, whether it is a nuclear family, an extended kinship, a neighborhood, or a church or synagogue. We feel the impact most strongly of those with whom we live or know intimately, yet their influence often goes unnoticed in society's effort to focus on ("blame") mothers.

Until recently, professionals and researchers minimized the influence of siblings. Recent studies, however, point to the lasting influence of brothers and sisters. Growing up, most children spend more time in the company of their brothers and sisters than their parents. One study of 140 siblings under the age of 7 found that brothers and sisters interacted with each other an average of eighty-five times per hour—even when mothers were available.[17] Marian Sandmaier, author of *Original Kin*, who interviewed eighty men and women for her book about adult sibling relationships, writes, "Nearly every individual I spoke with believed that a brother or sister had a major, enduring impact on some aspect of his or her personality development."[18]

I've seen this with my own children, particularly in the area of education and achievement. Andrew is bright and has done well academically, but he didn't identify with the achievers in high school. He didn't want to get involved in extracurricular activities and made fun of the kids who made honor roll. Growing up, Margot looked up to her big brother. I felt that she (unconsciously) held herself back academically and from getting involved in school activities to gain her brother's approval. During her senior year of high school, I saw how accurate my hunch had been. When Andrew left for college, Margot became an editor of the yearbook, her science project won a citywide contest, and her grades soared. Andrew's leaving freed her to do what she had wanted to do all along.

Fathers, too, leave their imprint on their children. Whether parents are living together, separated, or divorced, children deeply feel their father's presence—or absence. Many women talked about their husband's influence, particularly in disciplining the children.

My Turn

When I interviewed Stacey Hines, a 52-year-old woman who sells real estate and is married to Ray, an investor, she came across as an efficient, precise woman who is always in control. Her house was spotless, carefully decorated with expensive Early American furniture. She looked like the kind of woman whose kids did all the right things. As we talked, however, she painted a far different picture than the family I had imagined.

Stacey worries that the lives of her daughter, Deb, 25, and her son, Don, 19, are out of control. "My kids both drink entirely too much," she said. "Anytime we are away for a long evening, I know that I'll come home and find that either the police had been here, there had been some kind of party, or something happened that should not have. When Donnie is home on break, we're afraid to go out for dinner for more than an hour."

Both staunch, church-going Protestants, she and her husband have very different child-rearing philosophies. Stacey feels the kids need discipline; Ray is opposed to any rules and regulations. Because of what she calls his "macho-Texas" personality, she usually ended up going along with him, after much bickering. Each time their son totaled a car, for example, Ray replaced it with a new one. Stacey wanted to take away his license. Ray disagreed; their son just needed to sow his wild oats. Reflecting on her parenting now that the kids have left home, Stacey believes that they needed, and still need, discipline.

Other women spoke of their husband's positive influence on their children and their development. Gail Hart, a warm, outgoing woman, told me that her husband was very strict with their son and daughter when they were growing up, yet their kids adore him. "If you said to them, 'I know you love your parents equally, but who do you favor?' they would both say, 'My father,'" she says. "He's tough, but he's not mean. They respect him because he's so good to them." Her husband and their daughter, now 22, take a Spanish course together and go out to dinner once a week. "He just wanted to spend a night a week with her," says Gail, a smile spreading across her face. "He's a really great dad."

As our children become teenagers, they spend less and less time at home and become more involved with their peers. The increasing impact of friends during adolescence, however, does not necessarily mean a diminishing of parental influence, according to recent studies. Peer relationships broaden teens' emotional ties; in most cases, they do not replace parental connections. Parents and peers often complement each other and reinforce common goals or impact on different areas of a teen's life. For example, teenagers tend to discuss career and academic goals with parents while they prefer talking about dating and social concerns with their peers.[19]

We tend to think of peer influence as negative: that it's our kids' friends who push them to get involved in drugs, drinking, and sex. Sometimes they do, but research shows that adolescents affect each other negatively *and* positively. For example, while peers may influence teens to experiment in antisocial ways, they also provide support to stay clean and sober, excel academically, and stay in school.[20]

Realizing that we are not the only important influence on our children can help us put our mothering in perspective. Yes, we had a significant role but so did our children's siblings, father, and peers. All these influences shaped our children and in part determined who they are today.

COMING TO TERMS

Two years have passed since Andrew and Margot dropped out of college. During those two years, Dick and I have tried to give them the space to "find themselves" and to love them for themselves: two young adults trying to figure out who they are and how they fit in the world. We have supported them emotionally throughout this time—as our long-distance phone bills will attest—but we told them early on that we would not support them financially if they were not in school, and we did not.

Margot did take time off to follow the Grateful Dead. She traveled with friends, slept in vans, camped in parking lots. She supported herself by making dresses and selling them at concerts. She checked in with us each week and came home every few months to catch up on sleep, showers, and home cooking. After about nine months, the constant travel started to wear on her. She worked on an organic farm for several months, then felt ready to go back to school. She started slowly, taking a couple of courses to ease back into an academic environment. Now, more than a year later, she is in school full-time. She's there because she wants to be there. She's ready to learn, open to new ideas, and immersed in her studies. Her experiences outside the classroom have matured her; she has become a sensitive, caring young woman.

Andrew, too, has returned to school. In the interim he supported himself waiting tables, being a take-out chef, and working at a coffeehouse. He is learning where his talents and aptitudes lie. He has rediscovered reading, written powerful poetry, and mastered the computer and on-line services. He, too, has gained knowledge that he could not have learned in the classroom. Each day he grows in confidence and becomes more responsible. He's becoming a *mensch* and I'm proud of him.

These last two years have been a difficult learning experience for me. I've spent many sleepless nights and anxious days worrying about where my kids were or what they were doing. I've learned that I cannot control them, nor can I change them. They must live their own lives, make their own choices, and find what makes *them* tick.

Today I truly believe that a college education does not ensure happiness. It's far better for our children to understand themselves and to find out what satisfies them than to go through the motions of being students to please Dick and me and end up with hollow degrees.

I've also begun to question why it's so important for us *as parents* that our children stay in the mainstream and follow a traditional path. This concept is damaging to us, our children, and society because it promotes clones, discourages original thinking, and hampers creativity. We say we value independence, individuality, and resourcefulness, yet we're more comfortable when our kids follow the straight and narrow. In retrospect, I see my children's experiences as growth-enhancing and character-building. If I'd had that attitude several years ago, I could have saved myself a lot of angst.

I remind myself that the book is not closed on any of our children. Still young adults, they have many years of living ahead of them. It's true that their departure is a natural demarcation, a time to look at how they "turned out," but we must keep in mind that they are not finished products. They will continue to develop and grow in ways we cannot imagine today. We must have hope that they will find what they are looking for.

I also remind myself that the book is not closed for us as parents either. Our children are no longer living with us and we are not actively mothering, but we are still their parents. Our relationship with our children will change as they mature and we age, and we will have many opportunities to make up for what we feel we did wrong when they were younger. We cannot redo the past, but we can relate differently to them in the future. Our recognition that we may have failed our children in certain ways may motivate us to change our relationship now. It's not too late.

I now believe that I didn't cause my children's difficulties. Of course, I had an important part in their development, as did my husband. Part of who they have become are two children raised by Dick and me. But many other factors, over which I had no control, influenced them. I try not to dwell on the past and the "would've, could've, should'ves," and I'm also trying not to project too far into the future. I know now that their lives are a reflection of themselves, not of my mothering.

Some parents, however, know they have neglected their children because of the parent's own drug addiction, alcoholism, depression, or overwhelming personal problems. These women have wrestled with guilt and self-blame for years. Their inability to accept their own mistakes and their own imperfections can leave them paralyzed. Until they can convert their anger at themselves into self-compassion, growth will be impossible.[21] The past cannot be relived, but they can try to make amends with their young adult children and, most importantly, forgive themselves. Only then can they put the past behind them and move on with their lives.

THE RANDOMNESS OF LIFE

None of us sets out purposely to harm her children. Most of us do the best we can at our job of mothering. But ultimately, we have little control over what happens to our children or to ourselves. So many factors *unrelated to parenting* affect how we parent. How can we be even "good enough" mothers when our own mother is dying of cancer, we're going through a divorce, or we're working long hours? Or when we must cope with our own mood swings, stacks of debts, or an uninvolved husband? Our own mental health, as well as our ability to "be there" for our children, depends on so many factors working right and working together.

In addition, many things happen to our children that are beyond our control. One child chooses to hang out with the wrong crowd, another gets a chronic disease, a third has learning disabilities. As Anna Quindlen, former columnist for the *New York Times*, writes, "It's the randomness of it that is so awful. . . . Children step in front of cars and fall in pools; teenagers take the wrong drugs, drive too fast, dip too deep into some well of despair. Some get stuck in the tar of the bad spots, and some do not. Some grow up strong with bad upbringings, and some falter with good ones."[22] Somehow we think we can counteract the randomness if we try hard enough. We read books on parenting, listen to the experts, confer with our friends. "There is a big gap between knowing and doing," writes Judith Viorst in her book *Necessary Losses*, "because mature, aware people are imperfect too."[23] With all the right intentions, we can still fail our children. And inevitably, in some way, many of us have.

And so we must come to terms with the randomness of life—of our life, in particular. This is no easy task, this acceptance of things as they are and not as we want them or hoped they would be. We must come to terms with our part in how our child has turned out. We must reconcile that no matter how loving and caring and nurturing we think we have been, some of our children may not make it in the world,[24] and certainly many may not make it as we, their parents, had hoped and dreamed.

Part of the maturity and wisdom that we gain in middle age comes from our accepting what we cannot change. This means coming to terms with the fact that none of us have been perfect parents. It also means accepting—rather than trying to control or change—our children as separate human beings with their own strengths and limitations. We share this task with many, many women. Talking with close friends can help us gain acceptance. The solidarity and encouragement we receive from support groups, twelve-step programs, and psychotherapy can also help us come to terms with what we cannot alter in ourselves and in our children.

Our ultimate task, however, is to gain our self-esteem and our contentment from within, not from our children's achievements or their happiness. No one understands this better nor struggles with it more than women whose children are in recovery from substance abuse. A woman whose son is a recovering alcoholic said to me, "When I can have a good day no matter what my son is doing, I know I'm getting better." The more we all can put our mothering in perspective and put the focus back on ourselves, the better we'll feel—and the more we'll feel able and ready to embrace the next phase of our lives.

CHAPTER FOUR

SEPARATIONS AND LOSSES

At first glance, Sherri Halpern seems to have it all. Married to Stuart, a successful attorney, she lives in an exclusive development in the Pittsburgh suburbs. Their children, Michael, 24, and Heather, 20, are good kids. In fact, they are Sherri and Stuart's favorite couple to travel with because they have such fun and go along with whatever their parents want to do.

Sherri loved having her kids around the house: the phone ringing, the music blasting, their friends popping in and out. But her children never comprised her whole life. She owns an art gallery and treasures her leisure-time routines, including her morning walk and weekly tennis game with friends. And she loves entertaining.

Michael went out of town to college but moved home three years ago to attend a nearby law school—just as Heather left for college. Two months before I met Sherri, Michael moved into his own apartment, closer to school, about 30 minutes from his parents' suburban home. Sherri, who appeared so "together," began unraveling at once. She told me, "I thought I had my life together and that having a career was going to make it fine when my kids left. Having interests and hobbies, I figured that I always had a tremendous amount going for myself so that it would be easy for me when my children left. Well, the moving truck came, and I went down with Michael to set up his apartment, and as soon as I left his apartment. . . ."

She paused. "The tears were uncontrollable on the way home. I didn't know where they were coming from. It was just so much sadness, so much sadness. I felt like my life has changed, and it will never be the same. They are grown up, and they don't need me. They don't need me to cook their meals or make their beds or do their wash. I got home and told Stuart. Then I got into bed, I didn't want dinner, and I just cried." Sherri felt miserable for six weeks. She was weepy, let her appearance go, had no energy, didn't talk to her friends.

Sherri mourned for her children almost as though they had died. While certainly not a death, our children's departure is a loss, another loss at midlife. We've already said good-bye to our youthful looks, to our firm bodies, to our childbearing years. And now, our children leave home.

Grieving is a natural response to the loss of someone close to us. Not everyone is in touch with her grief at this time, nor do most of us express it as openly as Sherri. Her reaction to her children's leave-taking is part of her own unique story, but it touches broader themes that many women discussed with me. It is the story of how we face a variety of losses, some conscious and some unconscious, when our children leave home. It is about the role work plays in tempering, avoiding, and protecting us from the losses. It is about how separating from sons differs from separating from daughters and how some of us have difficulty letting go of either. Lastly, it is about how we need to come to terms with our losses before we can welcome the freedom that awaits us.

SO MANY LOSSES

Children bring activity, vitality, and busyness to a home. Picture this scene as I come home late one afternoon during Margot's spring break. As soon as I open the door, I hear the stereo blasting with sounds of the Grateful Dead. An aroma of curry permeates the house. I walk into the dining room; fabric, thread, and patterns cover the table. Margot stands at the kitchen counter, the phone to her ear, chopping carrots and green peppers. Brown rice steams on the stove. "Hi, Mom," she says with a smile, "I'll be off the phone soon."

When our children leave, the house may feel too quiet, dead, lifeless. More than anything else, women told me they missed their children's physical presence on a daily basis. Single parents, in particular, said they missed their children's companionship and conversation. "The hardest thing for me," said the divorced mother of two, "is not having their company and the company of their friends. It is more the companionship than the parenting, as such. I don't sit around with my friends and talk about books and ideas. The kids are still very idealistic—or completely cynical. They bring a different approach, a different kind of thinking than one's own peer group does."

Several women told me that they missed their daughters—but not their sons—on a visceral level. They longed for contact with their bodies: putting their arms around them, hugging and kissing them, cuddling in bed. Gina Ruland, a warm, expansive woman and the mother of a son and daughter in their early twenties, said, "I miss my daughter so profoundly that it is physical. Absolutely physical. I long for her. I pine for her. . . . It hurts. I never would have guessed that. I am not that active in my kids' lives. I am very proud of them and thrilled with them, but I don't live their lives. I am surprised at this longing." I understand this: At times I feel an overwhelming urge to hug Margot, 2,000 miles away.

Of course, not all women miss their children's presence. Those who did generally had positive relationships with them as teenagers. Women with large families and women who were strongly career-oriented felt primarily relief at their children's departure. Women with difficult or troubled teens were glad to have their kids out of the house and reprieved not to face their problems every day. That didn't mean that they had separated emotionally from their children. But the physical distance from their children helped the parents detach from their children's problems.

When our children leave home, we lose a critical role. No longer actively mothering, we become more peripheral to our children's lives. They don't need us in the same way. Although most teenagers lead fairly independent lives, home still remained their base and, in most cases, their hub. Even if they brushed us off or waved goodbye as they ran out the front door, we shared our daily lives with them. Unlike Sherri, who opened the chapter, most women told me they felt relieved to relinquish the physical aspects of their role: the cooking, washing, and carpooling. But they missed their role as nurturer, adviser, confidante, and protector.

For many of us, though, mothering encompasses more than a role: It comprises a large chunk of our identity. Just as a widow feels the loss of part of her identity after her husband's death, so we mothers question our identity with our children gone. Now we wonder: Who am I without my kids at home? And how will my new role, mothering young adults away from home, change the way I feel about myself? Questions of identity such as these typically affect people grieving for a lost loved one, according to Jungian psychotherapist Verena Kast. A grief reaction causes a shaking up of our established identity, she believes, and consequently, the search for a new identity. The grieving process requires us to rethink ourselves and shift from a "relationship-self" to an "individual-self." In doing this, we redefine our identity.[1]

Many of us struggle with this process: As our identity as a mother—our "relationship-self"—shifts, we need to discover or rediscover our "individual-self." But because this process is so unsettling, we often feel disjointed and confused. Sherri told me: "I felt like I was coming apart. I had every negative thought in the world about who I was and who I wasn't. I had no idea who I was. In yoga class during that time, I couldn't balance, everything was in such pain."

Sherri's body told her what she knew in her head and her heart: that her life felt out of sync. She felt unstable and unsteady, as though she were standing on one foot. Like many women, she struggled to figure out who she was now that a large portion of her identity and *raison d'etre* had been removed. How could she stabilize herself? Fill the void? Become whole again?

My Turn

With the end of active mothering, we also grieve, whether consciously or unconsciously, for the loss of *our own* childhoods. In *The Myth of the Bad Mother*, Jane Swigart explains how this happens when our children reach the end of their adolescence: ". . . through our children we stayed in close touch with our youth and those who loved us then. The immediate experience of our children allows us to recapture those intense, early relationships. When their childhood ends, whatever we did or did not get then is lost forever. There is a finality in the knowledge that our children cannot get it for us."[2]

A personal experience made me realize how I lost—forever—my own childhood when our children left for college. The first Jewish New Year they were both away at school, the holiday felt empty. I felt alone. I missed their banter, even their complaining about going to services, at our family dinner. But I also missed my parents, who had both passed away, *more* that particular year, and I longed for my cousins and aunts and uncles, most of whom were also dead. In my memory I still carried the vision of Nana and Papa, Lo and Uncle Don, Gladys, Lillian, Ted, and Marie, all sitting around the table, chatting in small groups after dinner, gathering around the fireplace, helping out in my mother's kitchen. *That* was a holiday, and I wanted that, I wanted *them*, for my children and for me. Usually we spend holiday dinners with my husband's family, which, of course, is not my own. Even before the children's departure, the holidays often evoked nostalgic childhood memories for me, but with Andrew and Margot gone, I felt particularly sad, knowing that I had lost forever all chance of recapturing those special times.

In the years since our children left home, however, I've tried to make the holidays special in a different way. I've realized that rituals matter to me personally, that I wasn't lighting candles or making honey cake *just for the children*. Like many women, I'm trying to create new rituals so the holidays remain meaningful, whether or not our children are home. For the last several years, we've invited a group of good friends—some empty nesters, some with children still in high school—over for a potluck holiday dinner. Everyone arrives, dressed for services, with a dish in hand. Seated around a long table, we say the blessings in unison, then have a lively discussion as we "ooh" and "aah" over each other's contributions. We all pitch in, serving dinner, clearing the table, filling the dishwasher. "What a special evening," everyone agrees as we head to services.

HOW LONG THE LONGING?

Not all women experienced these losses when their *last child* left home. Some of us had a harder time with our first child's leave-taking, because we had a special relationship with that particular child or because we felt that our oldest child's departure shattered the family unity. When the first of her two daughters went to college, one woman told me, "It just felt like we had this big hole in our family." A few women told me that their children going to college didn't feel like a real separation because they still came home for vacations and holidays; but when their children graduated, rented their own apartments, or moved to another part of the country, that felt permanent, more like "a severing of some kind of a tie," as another woman said.

Nor did all of us long for our children. Some women told me that they felt teary or cried when they dropped their last child off at college, but their sadness evaporated by the time they returned home. In fact, one woman told me she was surprised at how easily she moved on and how guilty she felt about it: "I thought it was going to be a horrendous phase of my life and instead, it has turned out to be wonderful," she said. "So in some ways, I feel that maybe

I am not a good mother, that maybe I am missing some piece of my heart or something, because maybe I should be missing them more."

In contrast, other women longed for their children for months, even years. A college professor who felt very attached to her son because of problems arising from his learning disabilities said, "When my son went away to college, I had a low-grade anguish. It was a sense of emotional loss and distance, which I had never had to deal with in my life before. It in no way prevented me from going through my normal routines, having my normal range of emotions, and so forth, but it felt like a low-grade lynching of a part of me." This anguish lasted a full year.

Another woman, an elementary school principal whose daughters have been out of the house for six years, still feels a void today. "It just seems *still* there's an emptiness of everything that went on here for all those years," she said. "As time goes on, it's less. You get used to your life as it is, so it's more distant and certainly not something I think about all of the time. But every so often, I think, 'Gee, it would be nice to have them around.'"

In contrast, several homemakers experienced a briefer and less intense grief than many career women did. "The anticipation was almost worse than the reality," said Sharon O'Malley, a bubbly stay-at-home mom with an active volunteer life. "The adjustment was faster than I thought—72 hours. I had anticipated the quiet house and that really bothered me, but you get up and do what you do. I told myself I had a full life before I had children, and, therefore, why not have an equally full life after they're raised and gone?"

Am I hearing right? A school principal and a college professor, women with interesting, engrossing careers, still long for their children years after they've left home? And yet a homemaker/ mother is doing just fine? I know the empty-nest syndrome does not exist, yet even *I* expected that women who have meaningful work would have an easier adjustment and feel the loss less. What role does work play, after all?

WORK: SALVATION OR DISAPPOINTMENT?

Much to my surprise, I found that women who work outside the home do not automatically feel the loss less than homemakers do, nor do working women necessarily have an easier time coming to terms with their children's departure. Of the forty-five women I interviewed, eight were traditional homemakers. Only one was not actively involved in volunteerism; the others put in from 20 to 40 hours a week and sometimes gave more time around a special event. So it could be said that nearly all of the women I interviewed "worked outside the home," because volunteer work played a role similar to paid work in the lives of women who did not hold salaried positions. While these women did not need to work for financial reasons, they felt as committed to their volunteer obligations as they would to a paid position. When their children left home, their volunteer commitments functioned, for them, the same way that paid work did for the employed women.

Just how did work, whether paid or volunteer, help us in accepting our losses? Almost every woman I spoke with told me that she knew that work would be important for her—*in some way*—in getting on with her life. Work was one aspect of our lives that we could regulate at a time when so many of our emotions seemed out of control. Work grounded us when so many parts of our lives seemed in flux. And work gave us a stable identity as we adjusted to shifts in our role as mothers and in our concept of ourselves as women.

My Turn

Our increased involvement in work and work-related activities took different forms. Of course, many of us went back for graduate degrees or special training when our last child left home. Those who did not seek more education took on more responsibility at the office, worked longer hours, or took on new and bigger projects.

In contrast, the few corporate women I interviewed told me they want *less* involvement in work, not more. Meg Finger, a product group manager at a multinational computer corporation and the divorced mother of three sons in their late twenties, reshuffles her priorities day by day. She worked in the computer industry until she got pregnant, then stayed home until her youngest was 12. Her divorce forced her back to work. She began with an entry-level position but has been promoted rapidly. Ten-hour days were the norm while her boys were in high school. She felt she had no choice if she wanted to send them to college. Her boys cooked dinner and did their own laundry, but she was still strung out. "I could have quit after they got out of college," she acknowledges, "but I was rising up the ladder; I was hooked."

But she didn't stay hooked for long. Today, she's disgusted with the whining, blaming, and dog-eat-dog atmosphere. "Some days I just walk out; I can't take it anymore. I think of leaving permanently, but I don't know what I'll do when I grow up." Meg admits the money would be hard to give up, but the awards—she won four last year—mean less and less to her. "Working is not as much fun as it used to be. It could be that the company is not doing that well, and I don't see a leader in upper management. But I think it's more that my priorities are changing. I never have time for my grandchildren, and I don't feel like I'm contributing in a *human being* way."

JUST HOW DOES WORK HELP?

It's understandable that those who were accustomed to leading full, active lives would want to stay busy and use work to fill up their empty hours. Women with fulfilling careers naturally chose to become more involved in work because they found it challenging and satisfying. But busyness can be difficult to distinguish from avoidance. Work can also serve as an escape, a way to avoid facing the emptiness at home or come to terms with the cauldron of emotions left in the pit of our stomachs after our children leave home.

When women threw themselves into new or more complicated projects, the extra activity and involvement did buffer their longing for their children. It also diverted their attention from the hole in their family to the fullness of a life they *could* build with their own hands, if they chose. This new involvement began to change their perception of themselves: They weren't just mothers without children at home, but women, full of promise, with an exciting opportunity ahead of them. Marti Smith illustrates how this transition works for many women. She is a long-time teacher who was offered the position of principal the year her daughter left for college. She grabbed the challenge, telling me, "I remember saying a whole lot that this was the best year to start this type of job, given it would really not allow me to spend time thinking about how much I missed her. It worked—for sure, that's what happened."

Accepting the principalship helped Marti shift into a new phase of her life and into a different way of seeing herself. She had always considered herself primarily a mother and a wife and for years thought of teaching as "a nice part-time job." But with her daughter's departure, she says, "I had to make some determinations. The primary force of my life was as a mother, and that wasn't there anymore, so I had to figure out who I was. I remember saying I need a career now, not a job. My new career as a principal helped me define who I am."

Marti did not slip on her new identity as easily as she walked into the principal's office. It took time to develop. When I interviewed her five years into her principalship, she said, "I'm not struggling with identity issues any more. I think by virtue of being in this position for this long, being successful, being seen by colleagues and friends as someone who is enmeshed in my career—it all helps. This is very, very strong for me. I still see myself as a mother and a wife *and* a career educator. So I don't question who I am anymore. That shift took place as I began to be successful in what I was doing."

The results of women's involvement or overinvolvement in work were not always as positive as Marti Smith's. Nor were the repercussions as they—or I—expected. Claudia Bickerson, for example, illustrates someone who substituted work for her children. The mother of three children, she considers herself a professional volunteer. When she was raising her children, she served as Girl Scout leader, Cub Scout leader, homeroom mother. When her last child left a year ago, Claudia "overweighted" herself with volunteer activities. She said to me, "I was just so busy. The telephone was ringing constantly, because I was fundraising here, on the board there, raising money for this organization. I was trying to get the strokes that I used to get from my kids from outside sources."

A rift at an organization she had formed fifteen years ago forced her to realize how she had tried to "parent" the organization now that her children were gone. Claudia explains, "I *built* this organization. All of a sudden I got slapped real hard in the face: They told me they didn't need me anymore. It absolutely devastated me. I quit cold, dropped off the board, furious, never had closure with anyone. But now I see it as a godsend: If I stayed, I'd still have been trying to parent this organization. It had become my child now; it was filling my nest." The organizational shake-up forced Claudia to examine how she treated her volunteer work almost as another child. The void she felt when she walked out, reminiscent of the pain she experienced when her last child left home, made her realize how profoundly she missed her own children. Now she is struggling to find a way to stay involved in organizations without becoming their mother.

Women also told me of their deep disappointment when their careers didn't protect them, as they hoped they would, from feeling devastated when their children left. "Work matters so much to me. So much of what I am is my work," admits the mother of two college students who does development for a university. "Work was always the way I could get my head on straight. But when I had this tumultuous time after Craig (her son) went to school, I just couldn't do it. *I just could not do it.*" "It" was an out-of-town presentation two weeks after Craig left for college. "I was driving to Chicago, weeping and wearing sunglasses. I had to do this presentation from noon till 4:00, and I did it. It wasn't that important. It wasn't that good either. I remember thinking, I should not expect my career to insulate me from that kind of emotion."

The women's movement had promised us that our careers would fulfill us. But that's not what many of us found. Now with our children gone, we feel disillusioned, angry, and disappointed. "The expectation was that the process of getting your life and a career together would fill you up to a point where you would have enough gratification in your work that it would fulfill you," says Sherri, the art gallery owner who opened the chapter. "Well, guess what? I've done it, and it's not where it's at. I thought that if I had a career, made extra money, and was independent—that's gonna do it, that's gonna make me really feel happy. I expected that when the children left, I'd have my career to make me happy.

"While I was parenting and had the career and the other things, I felt like I really had everything. I just felt happy and complete. But now that part has left; there is a void. "I realized that it wasn't the career that was doing 'it' necessarily. It really was the parenting that was going to my heart. And now I find a piece of the puzzle is missing."

I shared Sherri's disillusionment. I, too, thought that my career would protect me when our children left home. My work is engrossing and rewarding, but I still missed the kids. Work provided an escape and a respite, giving me an involvement in something I truly cared about. Work occupied me while I tried to sort out my feelings. When I was engaged in an interesting writing project, I lost myself in my writing. But during the inevitable slow times, when I was between assignments or waiting to hear from an editor about a new project, my thoughts would return to the void at home.

Even during the times my career flourished, though, I realized that my life lacked something. I knew the answer, for me, was not working longer and longer hours and taking on more and more assignments. It wasn't activity and busyness I yearned for. Like Sherri, I longed for that piece that went to my heart, that involvement that grabbed me emotionally. I knew, as did many others, that I needed something meaningful—besides my career—to sustain me and satisfy me in the years ahead.

Pulitzer Prize–winning columnist Ellen Goodman grappled with similar issues when her daughter left for college several years ago. She wrote, "A long time ago, I thought that mothers who also had work that engaged their time and energy might avoid the cliché of an empty-nest syndrome. A child's departure once meant a mother's forced retirement from her only job. Many of us assumed that work would help protect us from that void. Now I doubt it.

"Those of us who have worked two shifts, lived two roles, have no less investment in our identity as parents, no less connection to our children. No less love. No less sense of loss."[3]

If someone with a career as absorbing and satisfying as Ellen Goodman's can feel this way, it's no wonder that the rest of us also struggle with these issues.

A DIFFERENT KIND OF SEPARATION

Raising a daughter is very different from raising a son. We share a female body and a sexual identity with our daughters, which creates an intimacy that infuses every aspect of our relationship. Such identification does not exist between us and our sons; with them, we experience a sense of *otherness*.[4]

Separating is a normal part of our relationship with our sons.[5] From the moment of his birth, we know he's different. As he grows up, we try to nurture him while we encourage him to identify with his father or a father surrogate. To promote a healthy separation from us, we do our best to affirm his competence and effectiveness, says Evelyn Bassoff, Ph.D., in her book *Between Mothers and Sons*.[5] As he grows more confident and capable in his own right and in his own way, however, he still needs to come back to us for reassurances from time to time. According to Bassoff, we should try to respond warmly to his requests but continue to respect his need to create distance. Ideally, we recognize that separation is normal—not a rejection of us. When all goes well, we do not retaliate by abandoning him physically or emotionally or overindulge him to keep him close to satisfy our own needs.[6]

My Turn

When our sons leave home at the end of their adolescence, the emotional distancing continues. Because of the more permanent nature of this separation, however, it can be a difficult time, particularly for a single mother who has developed a close relationship with her son during the years she raised him alone. In her novel, *For Love*, Sue Miller follows Lottie Cameron, a middle-aged divorced mother of a college-aged son, during the summer she returns to her hometown to break up her deceased mother's house. Miller writes about how Lottie's second husband, Jack, teased her about her "romance" with her son, Ryan, whom she had raised single-handedly for years. Lottie consciously became involved with Jack when Ryan turned thirteen, because she thought a relationship with a man would help diffuse her attention from Ryan as he became an adolescent.

Nonetheless, it took his going to college for Lottie to recognize the end of the "mother-child romance." Miller writes of the losses Lottie felt and the changes she experienced as she separated from her son:

> What she'd felt in recent years, though, particularly since Ryan had gone off to college, was how absolute the ending to that mother-child romance was. It astonished her, given how central it had been to her life, given how much of her emotion had been taken up by Ryan—by love for him and anger at him and sadness with him and pride in him—how suddenly *gone* he was. All of that world was. She'd had a sense, the last few times he'd been home for a stretch, that there was some new relationship unfolding, something that, with luck, might look finally more like a kind of friendship. But mostly what she felt was the absence in herself of the old mothering emotions.

Not that she loved him less. Not that at all. But that the kind of love was different. Less consuming.

She was, on the whole, glad for this. But she missed the other too. She missed *him*, the person he had been and wasn't anymore. The younger Ryan, the little Ryan—all the little Ryans—who might as well have died, really. Sometimes she dreamed of him as he was at three, or six, and woke with a mixture of gratitude and bottomless sorrow—the same feeling she had when she dreamed of one of the few close friends she'd had who'd died.[8]

Whether we have sons or daughters, however, we experience a similar brew of feelings when our children grow up and move out. Separating from daughters, however, entails a very different process than separating from sons. While classic psychoanalytic theory holds that adolescents must break ties with their family to become their own person, more contemporary object relations theorists believe that daughters separate from their mothers while they continue to identify with them. Current feminist thinking supports this theory, stressing that girls don't truly "separate" from their mothers or sever the tie but learn to differentiate themselves from their mothers and grow within the mother-daughter relationship.[9] This doesn't mean our daughters stop speaking to us, cut us off, or lead lives isolated from us—any more than it does for our sons.

Most of our daughters do not want to break the tie but rather transform it and refashion it so that they are less dependent on us. They want a reciprocal relationship in which we respect them for whom they have become—individuals in their own right, not reflections of us, their mothers.[10]

MY TURN

In her earlier book, *Mothers and Daughters: Loving and Letting Go*, Evelyn Bassoff characterizes healthy separations as those in which mother and daughter have a *side-by-side* relationship. They remain close, but each has the freedom to live her life in her own way. The relationship remains strong because each brings her strength to the bond as a distinct individual. Those mothers and daughters who do not separate, Bassoff says, are trapped *one inside the other*. They crowd each other, and neither can move, let alone grow, without affecting the other.[11]

Much of the real separation work between us and our daughters begins during our daughter's adolescence when the little girl metamorphoses into a young woman and starts to assert her independence. Marcia Tepper illustrates how hard work during a daughter's adolescence can pay off later. A divorced mother and guidance counselor from Minneapolis, Marcia grew up with an alcoholic father and a mother who "never had her own life, a mother whose face was in my face all the time. Her life was my life. I hated that, and I wasn't going to do that to my kid." And, Emily, her only child, wouldn't let her do that. "My separation from her happened in high school because that's when she demanded it," explains Marcia. "I didn't have any choice then. We were going to kill each other or figure out how to live *separately* together." After hours and hours of therapy, both individually and together, they learned to respect each other's differences—in particular, the conflict between Marcia's need to plan ahead and Emily's spontaneous spirit.

"I used to have to know a month in advance what her plans were for Christmas vacation or in the morning what time she was going to be home that night. I learned to stop asking those questions. They weren't my problem," Marcia says. "Her coming home tonight is a perfect example of that. She told me that she'd be home tonight or tomorrow. (She's driving home from school for winter break.) The old me would have wanted to know: Is it going to be tonight? Should I have dinner? What do you want? I need to make plans. The new me: I didn't even ask when she was coming home. She just called and said, 'We're two hours away.' I said, 'Great.' That was that. I just accept her now, the way she is." And Emily does the same with her.

PHYSICAL DISTANCE/EMOTIONAL CLOSENESS?

Could she get any farther away?" That's the usual question people ask when I tell them that Margot goes to college in Washington State. What they really mean is "Could she get any farther away from *you*?" The truth is, at times it does feel like a personal affront that she doesn't want to live physically close to me. My feelings are compounded by public disapproval, particularly in a city like Philadelphia, where the children of many long-time residents live their entire lives within a few miles of their parents.

I understand Margot's desire to have a different experience in a new part of the country, but I still miss her and wish she lived closer. When I graduated from the University of Wisconsin, 2 hours from home, and applied to graduate schools, I wanted to move "out East" and live in a big city. I chose to attend the University of Pennsylvania in Philadelphia, where I've lived now for almost 30 years. Without kin nearby, I've developed close friendships that almost feel like family. Living near a city with a diverse population, I've had experiences I'd never encounter in a small Midwestern town. It's exciting to live within 30 minutes of a world-class orchestra and have scores of ethnic restaurants to choose from and easy access to Broadway shows.

Still, Margot and I would have an easier, more natural relationship if she lived close by. Sharing and communicating just happen when you spend time together. Each visit does not become an event, and expectations are more realistic. With phones, faxes, and e-mail, we try to stay close while living far apart, but it requires more effort and feels more artificial. Both Margot and I work to find quiet time to talk without distractions each week, so we stay connected.

WOMEN WHO CAN'T LET GO

The irony of motherhood is that it entails two seemingly opposite tasks: First, we try to create a unity with our child, and then, piece by piece, over years and years of parenting, we disassemble it.[12] Most of us have far more difficulty with the second task—that of letting go. When we hold on too long or too hard, we inhibit our child's development as well as our own.

Just *how* do some of us hang on emotionally when our children have physically left home? We stay involved, even enmeshed, in our children's lives by calling them at least once a day or seeing them several times a week if they live in the same town. We may live vicariously through our children, gaining status through their accomplishments, rather than pursuing our own. How often have we heard women talking of "my son, the doctor," or "my daughter, the attorney" rather than of themselves? Some of us continue to put our own lives on hold, so that if our child calls with a request, we cancel our plans and rush to fill the need. Even though we are now free to live our own lives, we don't. "I can't travel," we say. "The children might need me to babysit." Of course, we can all identify with bits and pieces of these situations, but for some women, these are the norm. Their lives have not changed since their children left home. While this can be a time of freedom, exploration, and self-discovery, women who haven't let go told me: "Everything's pretty much the same. Nothing's changed."

Just *why* do some of us cleave to our children? As we'll see later in this chapter, women hang on to sons and daughters for different reasons. But irrespective of the sex of their children, some mothers simply fear being alone; they feel abandoned when their children leave home. They need someone dependent on them in order to feel important and needed. Being alone, they feel isolated and frightened, wondering: How will I manage on my own? What will I do? How will I fill my time? No longer able to "hide" in a caretaking role, they face their ultimate aloneness, their mortality, when their children leave home. This prospect can feel so frightening that some women cling to their children in a last-ditch effort to salvage their former life or extend it beyond its normal span.

MOTHERS AND SONS

Logically, it would seem that we would have an easier time letting go of our sons, since we have been distancing ourselves from them for years. But in reality, many of us have difficulty letting go of our sons and giving up our caretaking roles. Jungian analyst M. Esther Harding suggests that we may keep our sons dependent on us because we fear losing our power, which comes from doing and, at times, "overdoing" for them. When we continue to take care of our sons when they are capable of doing the tasks themselves, however, we prevent them from becoming competent. At the same time, we keep them dependent on us and close to us.[13] If we do their wash, for example, they can't learn how take care of their own clothes. If we always cook for them, they won't learn how to make their own dinner.

Harding is right: Doing these chores makes us feel needed. Unfortunately, our behavior also keeps our sons dependent on us and prevents them from becoming competent in their own right. But there's another reason we fall back on our caretaking roles now: As our adolescent boys become young men, it's difficult for us women to find a role in relation to them and a way to connect with them as young adults. How many of us are comfortable talking about football or cars or rock music? With our daughters, it's easier. We share so much. With our sons, however, we may cling to our old, worn-out caretaking role because we want to stay connected to them, *but we don't know how.* We're unsure how to transform our relationship to a more mature, adult to adult-child connection. So rather than being left with nothing, we cling to a role that's familiar and comfortable. As we'll see in the next chapter, once we know how to carve out a more mature relationship with our sons, we'll be ready to give up our old way of relating.

The archetypical mother has two sides: one is soft, caring, and all-providing; the other, harsh, withholding, and firm, according to Harding. While we raise our children, we try to balance our hard and soft sides. Too much softness creates a dependent, helpless child; too much hardness leaves the child feeling alone and unloved. How tough to find this balance! As our child becomes an adolescent and eventually moves out, however, our task becomes even tougher: We must let our "hard" side predominate so our sons can develop into competent, capable men. Being "hard," for example, means insisting they pay us back when they borrow money or requiring them to make their own airplane or train reservations, rather than doing it for them. While these actions may feel uncaring to our sons, they, in fact, allow them to become more competent and take more responsibility for themselves. When this runs smoothly, we free our sons from a dependent position and, at the same time, liberate ourselves from the caretaking role.[14]

Not all women, however, want to be free of this role. Olympia Petronis is a 54-year-old woman who holds on tightly to her "soft" side. She gets great pleasure from taking care of her "boys," ages 21 and 22. She feels needed, wanted, and important. Olympia grew up in New York City, the only child of Greek immigrants. After high school and a stint at secretarial school, she married her high school sweetheart and moved to Baltimore, where they settled and raised a family. Olympia stayed home with her sons until they attended high school, then got a job as an administrative assistant for a small preschool in the neighborhood to help pay their college tuition.

Olympia spoke quietly and with little emotion as she told me how she still misses her sons' presence around the house—their lively family dinners, their teasing her—and how she felt "numb" the year her younger son left home. In our interview, she recalled her own school days: "When I went to school, my mother gave me a token for the subway, and I came home at night. School didn't break up our family. When you got married, you left the house. That's the way it was. I know times have changed, but that's the way it was."

Then she shifted to the present: "I knew I was going to miss them. I would rather have had them around at a local school. I know some women say, 'I'm tired of making dinners,' 'I'm glad they're out,' 'Now I have some time for myself.' That never crossed my mind. In fact, every time one of them calls, it's like 'When are you coming home, honey?' To this day, I'm glad when they're around."

My Turn

A little later in our interview, I asked Olympia if she still felt like a mother now that she was not actively parenting. She replied, "Oh, yes, because I am still out there working toward their education. As far as I'm concerned, I am still mothering them. I'm not changing diapers, but I am still working toward their future."

With the boys out of the house, Olympia continues to hold her 40-hour-a-week job. Usually, she comes straight home from work, unless she stops at the supermarket, and makes dinner every night for herself and her husband. When he travels for business, she'll stop and browse at a department store after work. She talks to one son almost every day and chats with the other several times a week. If she doesn't talk once a week to both boys, she gets "edgy." She continues to be active in her church and has a few close friends but no hobbies. "I used to read quite a bit and do a lot more baking," she says, "but I don't have time for those things anymore. Everything is kind of streamlined."

Olympia is a woman who can't let go. Her life hasn't changed since her sons left home. She continues to put her sons and her husband first and denies any needs of her own. Hanging on to her role as caretaker and nurturer prevents her from using this time for herself. It also hinders her sons from leaving freely, because they may feel guilty for taking away her caretaking role. When a woman leads her own life, it gives her children permission to do the same.

To understand Olympia further, however, it helps to look at her role in their family and the choices she made within the context of her ethnic background. According to Monica McGoldrick, a renowned family therapist who studied extensively the influence of ethnicity on families, Olympia has followed the prescribed orientation for Greek-American women: Family life is close and child-centered. A woman belongs in the home and gains fulfillment and status within the community through motherhood.[15]

For Olympia to challenge this traditional course would create internal conflicts and dissension within her family. Olympia has not and probably will not develop herself as an individual. She may never develop her own identity apart from her roles as mother and wife. But she is not discontent. She has the support of the Greek-American community, the only community that matters to her, and she receives far more strokes for continuing her caretaking role than she would if she went back to school, opened a business, or took up painting. True, Olympia has not let go. But we need to see her, and all women, within a broader context, so we can understand fully their roles, decisions, and choices.

MOTHERS AND DAUGHTERS

Middle-aged women who are overly attached to their mothers have difficulty letting go of their daughters. When I read that concept, or variations of it, in several psychology texts, it confused me: How could a mature woman who set up her own household, raised her children for almost twenty years, built a marriage, and may have survived a divorce still be so attached to her own mother? And just how could that relationship negatively affect her connection with her daughter?

As I continued reading and analyzed my interviews in this light, I realized that I had focused on the outward signs of independence—the house, the marriage, the children—and not on how a woman felt internally. When I read *The Dance of Anger*, the concept began making more sense. In the book, psychologist Harriet Goldhor Lerner explains that the task of defining and maintaining a separate self in our close relationships *begins* with our parents but does not end there. "Renegotiating relationships with persons on our own family tree yields especially rich rewards," she writes, "because

117

the degree of self that we carve out in this arena will greatly influence the nature of our current relationships."[16] In other words, if we do not resolve issues in one generation, we pass them on to the next. More specifically, if we don't separate emotionally from our mothers, we will hold on to our daughters. Then neither we nor our daughters are free to grow.

To be separate and independent from our mothers, however, does not mean we become emotionally distant from them. Rather, independence means that we clearly define our own selves on emotionally important issues, but it does not mean emotional distance.[17] We can be independent and still feel close and caring. We can live 2,000 miles apart and still feel connected. We can have our own opinions, feelings, and ways of doing things as well as the freedom to assert ourselves and differ with our mothers without feeling frightened or devastated. Ideally, we and our mothers live our lives side-by-side, to use Bassoff's term, not one inside the other.

I saw firsthand in my interviews that women who couldn't let go of their daughters had not separated from their own mothers. Gail Miller is an example of a woman so involved in her daughter's and her mother's lives that she has little separate existence of her own. She is a 56-year-old Jewish woman who taught school until her daughter, Melissa, now 22, was born. She stayed home, in part, because of health problems, which she described vaguely as "a little heart thing." Primarily, though, she felt and still feels that "if you are going to be a parent, you should be a parent." For Gail, that meant giving up all her outside activities, which included teaching, taking courses, and singing in the synagogue choir. She and her husband, Ted, also a teacher, used to go to concerts and the theater but gave up both when they became parents.

Gail lives in Boston, about six blocks from the house she was born in; Ted was also born and raised in Boston. Melissa is a senior at Boston University. As a young child, Melissa was very shy and cried every time she left her mother. In fact, Gail started a precedent of parents in her neighborhood remaining with their children at birthday parties, because Melissa wouldn't stay alone. Gail and Melissa remained tight until Melissa's senior year of high school; that year, they argued about everything. "Everybody told me we fought because she was leaving, and I didn't want her to leave," says Gail, acknowledging the truth in her friends' comments. "When Melissa started college, I thought I was going to be just devastated; so did everybody that knew me. 'Oh, God,' they said, 'Gail is going to end up in an asylum.' Melissa and I were very close. We did things together, we got along well, we always talked, so I was afraid that I would be lost when she moved on campus."

But instead, Gail did just fine: She slept better, worried less. But her life remained the same during the last four years. "My life still revolves a lot around Melissa," she says. "I spend lots of time getting her birthday presents and Hanukkah gifts, things like that. If she needs help with something, I am available to help her." They talk several times a week and usually get together once a week. When Melissa has free time, she and her mother like to go shopping together. When Melissa broke up with her boyfriend last year, Gail took her out every weekend to keep her busy.

Gail's mother, who is 85 and in failing health, also occupies much of Gail's time. She visits her mother several times a week, pays her bills, and keeps an eye on her mother's companion. Before she became ill, she saw her mother "a lot." They always got along fine, Gail says, except for an "underlying thing—she's so perfect. She could do everything and do it well. And she used to tell me what to do, which I resented."

Gail's relationship with her husband has not changed since Melissa left. He works evenings at the local health club, so they don't have much free time. "We're both homebodies," she says. Gail was the only homemaker I interviewed who was not involved in volunteer activities. She spends her free time reading, listening to classical music, or just wandering through town.

Is she happy? "Yeah," she answers with a huge sigh. "But it's a very boring life. I guess I could be happier, but I'm not unhappy. I've made peace with the way my life is, so it's OK, I guess."

Gail is stuck. Hanging onto her mother and to her daughter, she can barely move, let alone grow. Even her relationship with her husband is stagnant. It hasn't gotten better as many do when the children leave, and it hasn't gotten worse as some do when husbands and wives face each other without the distraction of children. Gail says she's made peace, but the "I guess" she tacked on to the end of her reply makes me wonder whether she truly has.

Gail has many years ahead of her that could be rich and fulfilling. But she has chosen to stay the course. Of course, she has her own reasons for not making changes, which are worthy of our respect. This is the best she can do at this time. It helps to keep the words of psychologist Lerner in mind: "Change requires courage, but the failure to change does not signify the lack of it."[18] We all have choices about whether we want to or are ready to change. It is not helpful to put *our* expectations on others. As we'll see in chapter six, personal fears and anxieties about how change will affect us and our relationships hold many women back from moving ahead.

Nancy Friday, author of *My Mother/My Self*, struggled for years to separate from her own mother. Only in researching her book did she learn: "The more I grow away from her and define myself, the more I see in her this other person she was before she became Nancy Friday's mother," she writes in the conclusion. "That is the magic: not that we can ever recreate that nirvana of love that may or may not have existed between us as mother-and-child, but that once we have separated we can give each other life, extra life, each out of the abundance of her own."[19]

LETTING GO

O ur children's departure from home reminds us of earlier separations. Yet very few of the women I interviewed thought that earlier separations prepared them for the enormity or the repercussions of the present milestone. Women knew that trips, overnight camp, and hospitalizations were temporary. With so-called normal, expected markers, such as our child's entrance into nursery school, kindergarten, or even high school—difficult as they were for some of us—we knew that our child would return home that very evening. The finality and implications that accompanied the current leave-taking accounted for our more profound feelings of loss and the grieving that resulted.

How can we come to terms with our loss? Many of us are familiar with the five stages of grieving that Elizabeth Kubler-Ross set out in her groundbreaking book, *On Death and Dying*: denial, anger, bargaining, depression, and acceptance. Recognizing these stages helps us remember that grieving is a process and that we all go through that process in our own way and at our own pace. This process, however, is not necessarily logical or orderly. You may feel fine now and think, "Whew! The worst is over," and then get a teary phone call from your daughter that sends you into a pit of depression. Your feelings will change, from day to day, even from hour to hour. If your child has just left for college and you feel absolutely forlorn, keep in mind that you won't always feel so awful.

MY TURN

Tell yourself: "This, too, will pass." Of course, your feelings are intense and fresh now, but they will change as you adjust to a life without children at home.

Try to accept *your* process, whatever it is. You can't shorten it or sidetrack it. Try not to fight it or to compare yourself to one of your friends. Each of our situations is unique. We all have our own particular relationships with our children and our own ways of handling loss. There is no wrong or right way.

To get a handle on your reactions to your last child's departure, consider, too, how you've coped with other losses in the past, such as the death of a parent or grandparent. Did you fall apart? Bury yourself in your work? Strike out at your husband or kids? We all have different capacities and ways of coping. Understanding that your present reaction is typical of the way you react to loss may help you be more understanding and more patient with yourself.

Not only does everyone go through the process in her own way, but the course of each person's mourning differs, depending on so many factors. For example, if you have prepared yourself for your last child's departure, you'll probably have an easier adjustment to her actual leave-taking. That is, if you started thinking about yourself and how you want to live without children at home while they're still in high school, you will be more prepared mentally and psychologically for the time when they actually leave. If you have taken steps toward making changes happen, you will be in even better shape.

The nature of your relationship with your child or children will also help determine how easy it is for you to let go. For example, a relationship that is overly dependent or plagued with unfinished business is harder to let go than a more harmonious one.[20] Like many women who were disappointed in their children, I realize now that my own unfinished business prevented me from letting go. I held on, in part, because I wasn't ready to relinquish my mothering role. The kids were out of the house, but I didn't feel good about the job I had done. If I held on, I reasoned, I could keep trying to do it better. As I saw them changing and growing, however, I realized that they *were* moving ahead, in their own way and in their own time, and that if I could let go and trust them and the process, they would be just fine.

I grieved for the children I did not have—those preppy mainstream kids, Joe and Jane College, who dress like ads for The Gap and attend and cheer at football games. Yet why should I have expected our children to squeeze themselves into a traditional mold when we'd always encouraged them to think for themselves and make decisions that felt right for them rather than follow the crowd? I now see Andrew and Margot as two bright, independent, resourceful kids who are struggling to forge their own lives. When I began to look at them as individuals with their own strengths, values, and dreams, it helped me separate and start letting go. I could then concentrate on myself and explore what I wanted to do in the years ahead.

While we share many commonalities, each of us has her own particular struggle. Sherri Halpern, who opened this chapter, withdrew from friends and activities so she could literally mourn for her children. It took her six weeks before she was able to move on. Then one day, she woke up and decided to take action. "I started calling friends and sharing what I had been going through, how I was feeling. Just talking about it has made a difference," she said. "I started to think like it's okay to feel good and not have the kids here."

Sherri realized later that she had such a rough time when her son left home because she was grieving for other losses as well. She had not mourned for her parents who were killed in a car crash the previous summer. In addition, one of her best friends had moved cross country over the summer. She felt abandoned—by her parents, her children, and her friend. As Sherri allowed herself to grieve for her children, she healed all these losses.

Sherri *experienced* her emotions. She let herself feel sad, abandoned, and alone. She didn't bury herself in her work, nor did she repress her emotions or deny them, as did some women who said, "Nothing's changed since the children left." We need to express our feelings and integrate them before we can move on. If we don't, our emotions may resurface in strange ways: through physical ailments, such as ulcers, headaches, or weight gain, or through psychological symptoms, such as anxiety, insomnia, or depression.

Of course, we all have different ways of getting in touch with and expressing our feelings. Many women find it helpful to keep a journal. Putting your thoughts and emotions on paper is a legitimate way to express them. In fact, studies have shown that writing about your feelings produces the same results as talking about them. If you can't fall asleep at night or wake up early, have your journal handy so you can get rid of the noise in your head that's interfering with your sleep.

Many women credited the support of good friends, particularly those who were also going through this transition, as key in moving on. With our children gone and our parents failing or dying, our contemporaries' support helps us feel less alone and less abandoned. Just having someone to listen to us and accept our feelings without making judgments helps us claim our own emotions. We feel validated when our peers confirm our feelings as normal and common and assure us that these, too, will pass. Talking with friends also reaffirms our sometimes shaky belief that our young adult children should be on their own and out of our houses—for our children's sake and our own. Friends with older children who have made positive changes in their lives can give us permission to do the same and reassure us that the best is yet to come. Friends aren't just for talking, though. They help enrich our lives by sharing holidays with us, spending weekends and evenings together, and just "being there" when we need them.

Some of you may be saying to yourself, "I'm not grieving at all. I'm OK. Everything's fine." And everything may be fine. Accept that and enjoy it. However, if you are a woman who says, "Nothing has changed in my life or my relationships," you may be denying the significance of your children's departure. It may be too painful to face just yet. You may fear that acknowledging the loss may force you to make changes in your life. And you're not ready for that. Accept where you are now, but also be aware that other emotions may be simmering beneath the surface. When you're ready, you'll acknowledge them.

For many of us, the passage of time also helps ease the transition, as does the knowledge that most of our children are coping just fine without us, their parents, looking over their shoulders, giving advice or reining them in. In our heart of hearts, most of us know today that we would not want our children back home. Nor do we want to do full-time nurturing anymore.

Once we've begun to detach, we will start to see our sons and daughters as young adults with hearts and minds of their own, not as extensions of ourselves or personal-need satisfiers. Our letting go frees them and liberates us. It opens up an opportunity to refashion our connections with our children to meet *their* needs as young adults and *our* needs as women without children at home.

CHAPTER FIVE

REDEFINING RELATIONSHIPS

"How's the book going, Mom?" Margot asks every time we talk. This may sound like a simple question, yet it signifies a major change in our relationship. In the past, as the parent, I asked the questions: "How's school going?" "How's the boyfriend?" "What's new?" But within the last year or so, she has started querying me about my life: "How was *your* weekend?" "What have *you* been up to?"

This shift is meaningful because it acknowledges that Margot sees me as a person, not just a mother, and that she recognizes I have a life beyond parenthood. Most importantly, it signifies that she wants a different kind of relationship with me now that she is a 21-year-old living on the opposite side of the country. I try to respond openly and honestly to her questions, because I too wish to develop a more adult-to-adult relationship with her. I want a candid, intimate, and authentic relationship—the kind most of us never had with our own mothers.

One day when we were talking, Margot suggested I read a book by a feminist whom she liked—another subtle modification in our relationship. For years my sister and I have recommended books to each other, and we still do. Hardly a month goes by that one of us doesn't say, "Have you read . . . ?" or "Have you heard about so-and-so's latest book?" When Margot suggested that book, I realized that our tie was taking on more and more qualities of a peer relationship. Since then, I have also suggested to her books that I've enjoyed. Savoring reading and liking the same books put us on equal footing: We are becoming intellectual comrades.

With our children's leave-taking, the dynamics of our significant relationships shift. No longer actively parenting on a daily basis, we have to learn to connect to our children in a different way and determine what kind of role we'll play in their young adult lives. The startling reality is that we will relate longer to our sons and daughters as adults than as children. And because most of us married women will outlive our husbands due to women's longer life span, our relationship with our adult children probably will be one of the most enduring of our lives. For all these reasons, we need to find new ways to connect with them and to show our love and affection without control or dependence.

Our children's leave-taking transforms our relationships with our husbands too. Some marriages can't survive without children as a buffer, while others develop new, deeper levels of intimacy. In addition, friendships take on added importance for many women, particularly those who are divorced or widowed.

In all of these significant relationships, we struggle to balance our need for intimacy with our desire for independence, to be part of a "we" yet maintain our sense of "I."[1] For some, the seesaw has tilted in favor of the "we" for far too long. Now, understanding the implications of our children's departure and recognizing that our lives are finite, many of us feel a greater need to develop meaningful, balanced connections. We don't have the patience for superficial chatter, we have less need for social approval, we want to get to the "nitty-gritty." We become more selective about where we put our energy so that each of our connections feels personally satisfying. To achieve that goal, we need to redefine our relationships.

A DIFFERENT KIND OF PARENTING

I had this incredible moment when Jim was graduating from high school," recalls Trish Palmer, the mother of a son and daughter in college. "He is a really competent kid. I wondered how he could possibly need me anymore or how I could be important in his life. The nice thing was he told me what he wanted. He told me that my knowing who he was was important, as was my accepting who he was, and that he wanted me to be available when things got hard. I just sat there, stunned, as he spelled out what the relationship was going to look like," Trish says, still thrilled four years after their conversation at Jim's ability to articulate what he needed from her as he matured.

My Turn

Most young adults do not express their needs so clearly, nor do we, their parents, always verbalize ours. Because we have arrived at a new, untested stage in our relationship, we have to maneuver and shift until we find a comfortable fit with each other. Our children are no longer adolescents, yet they are not quite adults either. What is our role now? How do we stay connected with our children without intruding on their space or trying to control their lives? What do they want from us? And what can we give them?

Sandi Kramer asks herself these questions often as she tries to figure out her role now that her three children have left home. Sandi is a homemaker from Houston who does volunteer fund raising, often putting in a 40-hour week. She has always been overly involved in her three children's lives by her own admission. When they were growing up, she was the Cub Scout leader, the homeroom mother, the one who brought drug and alcohol awareness to the schools. Her children never complained about her involvement—until recently. Sandi told me, "Josh, my middle son, disappoints me because he has pulled away from me. I think I understand what's going on, but it's real hard for me. He doesn't understand how much fun it can be to be close. He's engaged to a darling girl, Jill. I think he feels that I come on too strong for Jill.

"My husband and I are almost too giving, and people just don't understand. Want your house cleaned? We'd love to do it. We laid our other son's hardwood floors. We're always doing stuff like that. But we can be *too much* in their lives," she acknowledges. "I'm working on really pulling back, even though we have more fun with our kids than we do with our friends.

While Sandi feels she gives out of the goodness of her heart, Josh may wonder whether invisible strings are attached. He may feel guilty when he turns down a request of hers *because* she has given so freely. She, on the other hand, unconsciously may expect him to respond as she wishes, also because she has given so freely. While she probably wouldn't say it, she might be thinking: After all I've done for you, you can at least do this for me. Or one day she may call in her chit.

Thus, what feels like a comfortable involvement to Sandi feels excessive and intrusive to her son. She needs to pull back, or he may retreat even further. We all need to take seriously the clues our children give us about how much involvement is enough. Sometimes they tell us in no uncertain words: "Back off." At other times they are more subtle: They put off our visits, return our phone calls three days later, or give us excuses about why we can't get together.

Many of us are realizing that our other ways of "giving"— issuing warnings, offering suggestions, posing questions—can also feel controlling to young adults. Learning to keep our mouths shut and listen nonjudgmentally without giving advice or preaching—as hard as it is—shows our twenty-something sons and daughters that we have faith in their abilities and their decision making. Protecting our adult children doesn't make them stronger or enable them to take responsibility for themselves, we now know. They must make their own mistakes and learn from the consequences—as we sit by, with our hearts in our hands, and watch.

From the time our children were infants, many of us have struggled with holding on and letting go, with staying close and separating. Finding a balance doesn't get any easier as they get older. Physically, they're out of our houses, but emotionally we're still attached—as we should be and want to be. Now, we need different ways of relating, different ways of connecting with our sons and daughters. But ultimately with both, we strive for an interdependent relationship, based on mutual caring and respect for our differences.

My Turn

MOTHERS AND DAUGHTERS

Ironically, we may be drawn to our daughters because we are both struggling with similar issues—separation and self-definition—though from the different vantage points of midlife and late adolescence or young adulthood. (Because children are taking longer to complete college today, experts view the early twenties as late adolescence.) Our daughters are trying to develop a separate identity from ours while we are attempting to emotionally let go of our children and rediscover ourselves. We are both moving beyond the safety and security of our families, trying to establish independent identities apart from the (family) roles we've played in the past. Of course, we possess a more seasoned view of the world and feel time slipping through our fingers like sand. This realization may cause us to envy our daughters' youth, options, and idealism at times. But ideally, we support our daughters' growth and they ours.

These commonalities are particularly striking among widowed and divorced women and their daughters. A 51-year-old psychologist who was recently widowed remarked on how comfortable she feels with Sari, her 22-year-old daughter, and her friends: "I feel increasingly *uncomfortable* being with married couples now. But when I'm with single people, there's the sense of freedom or permission to be freer in some way—that's where I am. I've talked about this with Sari; she and all her friends think I'm very cool. I think they think I'm cool because I'm sort of like them.

"In some ways, I'm the same age as Sari. She's discovering the world for the first time, and so am I. She's dating, I'm dating. She's going to clubs, I'm going to clubs. She's finding her way, making a living, having a job, paying for car insurance, and I'm doing all these things too. So while I bring an extra twenty-five years to the experience, in some ways our lives right now are very parallel."

We also share parallel work lives with our daughters. In most fields, women, whatever their age, are working in predominantly male environments, trying to advance in a man's world. With far more working and living experience than our daughters, we can serve as informal mentors and role models for our daughters. An admissions counselor told me how her daughter often comes to her with questions about how to act in the workplace: "She'll ask me, 'How do you supervise without being bossy? Should I socialize with my coworkers? How do I tell my boss I hate part of my job?' We often discuss questions like these, while my son is more likely to go to his father."

Yes, these commonalities draw us to our young adult daughters. But here's the rub: Our daughters need to separate from *us* to become their own person, and we must let go of *them* to find our true selves at midlife. We're going through similar processes, yet the object of our separation is each other. How do we stay connected but separate? How do we each become a woman in our own right yet acknowledge the richness of our shared history? And how do we progress to a more egalitarian, mature kind of connection?

The issue of acceptance is crucial here. If we can accept ourselves, faults and all, and accept our daughters as imperfect as well, then we can move beyond the stereotypes and fantasies we carried of each other. Our shared gender and our strong identification make this particularly difficult. Yet we have to give up the notion that our daughters will be perfect, loyal young women, just as they must come to see us realistically. We cannot meet all their needs, nor they ours. We will disappoint each other at times; we can't always "be there" for each other. Acknowledging and accepting our limitations is a way of separating. It does not mean that we grow distant emotionally. Rather, we can now build a new, richer connection as two strong adult women.

My Turn

MOTHERS AND SONS

Typically, we do not share the same commonalities with our sons as we do with our daughters. We feel cultural pressure to distance ourselves, lest we end up with "mommy's boys." We're very careful not to intrude in their lives and to respect their boundaries. Yet my own experience, as well as that of my friends and my interviewees, tells me that we care deeply about our relationships with our young adult sons. We want to remain in their lives, to find a way to show our caring and concern that respects our sons' differences and their need for distance from us.

Young men need connection just as women do. We see how young men gravitate to fraternities, to college sports, and to relationships with young women as soon as they move out. They are searching for connection. These are ways for them to separate from us; they are not rejecting us.

Our task now is to find a way to stay connected with our sons that's acceptable to them and gratifying for us. Yes, we must give up our caretaking roles: We don't want our sons dependent on us for housekeeping chores. We can show our love now by being empathic, encouraging, and affirming.[2]

I try to do this in my relationship with Andrew, now 23. Our situation is complicated by the fact that he has moved back home temporarily. It seems much easier for mothers to keep their distance when their sons are out of their houses. But living at home, it's tempting to fall into old roles—me, the parent, taking care of him, the child—but neither of us consciously wants that. I refuse to do his wash or clean his room. I make an effort to treat him as an adult and to encourage his independence. I try not to give advice unless asked; I limit my questions. As a result, we have a comfortable give-and-take. I don't pretend to share his love of football and baseball, but we enjoy a similar sense of humor, we like talking about ideas and books, and we're often on the same wavelength in our perceptions about people.

BUILDING NEW BONDS

If we can separate emotionally from our children and respect their decisions about how they want to live their lives, we may be rewarded with their friendship. That doesn't mean that we're buddies. We're still their mothers and that implies some hierarchy, but our relationship can take on more of the qualities of a very special friendship: one fashioned by our family history and steeped in the intimacy of living together for eighteen years. Vivian Greenberg, author of *Children of a Certain Age*, suggests that the only relationship that makes sense as parents age and children mature is one of "filial friendship," because kin cannot be "just friends." As in any friendship, there are things that parents and children can't and shouldn't tell each other. On the other hand, there are some things that *only* parents and children *can* tell each other. But the criteria for friendship—acceptance, respect, affection, openness—are all there, Greenberg believes.[3]

The resulting adult-to-adult relationship can be mutually supportive—a new phenomenon for most of us. I remember the first time I experienced this: One day about a year ago I was having difficulty with a particular writing assignment when Margot happened to call. When she asked how I was doing, I told her how I was struggling to get this story right. She listened carefully, and when I finished talking, she said with feeling, "I'm sorry, Mom." The first time this happened I was taken aback. When it happened again and again, I felt pleased to know that she could "be there" for me, just as I had supported her over the years when she needed it.

My Turn

A college professor told me how she counted on her children, almost too much, when she was going through her divorce. "I leaned on them probably more heavily than I should have, but we were a very close family unit. No one else—not even my therapist—could understand or had experienced that family unit." Other women, too, expressed the sentiment that only someone who has lived in your family can understand the dynamics of your particular experience—how your husband withdraws when he's upset, how your son teases your daughter, the repercussions when you get angry. Living through these experiences creates a special bond.

Knowing that we can be honest and open with our children can be freeing. "One of the things I'm learning about myself is how I was not willing to show anger or upset at home," said the gallery owner from Pittsburgh. "I'd tone down my real feelings for fear that it would upset everybody. I wanted them to be happy. I didn't want them to see me upset or having a hard time. I guess I wanted to protect them.

"Now I want to share with my children. I feel that they are old enough to support me too. I'm there for them, and they can be there for me too. I think it's important for our children to give to us. After my son left for college, I told my daughter how sad and upset I was, how I cried the whole way home. I just told her exactly how I felt. It was really releasing."

How can we achieve this kind of mutually supportive, open relationship with our young adult kids? It takes work, mostly on our part, to modify the way *we* relate and respond to our sons and daughters. Consider the following options as a way to begin changing your relationship:

Advise, don't criticize. We wouldn't criticize a friend, yet we have no qualms about chastising our kids for arriving too late, dressing too sloppily, or spending too freely. We assume our way is better, and we know what's best for them. Who wants to be with someone who constantly finds fault or puts them down? Certainly not young adults trying to gain their own sense of self and develop confidence in their abilities.

Instead, be an adviser. Say nothing until asked. Then give your opinion, and let your children make their decision. If you have an open relationship—and they're willing—you can have a freewheeling discussion about their choices. If not, give your advice and say no more, except to reassure them that you know they will make the right decision. Then accept their decision—whatever it is. If it turns out wrong, don't say "I told you so." Let it be.

Bag the guilt. I don't know a single mother who wouldn't like her children to call her more often. But making them feel guilty for not calling doesn't encourage them to talk to us more frequently. They'll feel like calling less often if they know they will be reprimanded every time they call.

Instead of focusing on what you *should* be getting but can't, focus on what *you* need for yourself and on how you *can* get that. For example, if you need to touch base with your daughter once a week, tell her directly: "It important to me that we talk every week." Then discuss scheduling the calls. In this way, you are taking charge—you'll feel less helpless. You are directly addressing your needs; you are not manipulating her in a backhanded manner nor are you treating her like a child. You are also modeling a way for her to assert herself.

Live in the present, but heal the past. Changes in relationships take time and patience. Evolving from a parent-child to an adult–adult child connection will probably take years. It will take longer if your child still feels angry or hurt about something you did in the past. Yes, it's over and cannot be redone, but if your child still ruminates about it, you must address the issues.

Try to open a dialogue and just listen. He may still be furious about the time you didn't allow him to take the senior class ski trip or the way you yelled at him in front of his friends. Or she may have a deeper grievance, such as a long-standing sense that she felt second best compared to her brother. Whatever it is, listen without getting defensive. When they have said their piece, try to tell them what was going on for you when you committed this grievance. Discussions like these—and you will probably need more than one—will help free you both of the past, so you can move to a new level in your relationship.

When we relate to our children as adults, we'll find that they will want to share more of their lives with us. In fact, many women told me how their children as young adults enriched their lives. "I have developed a lot of new interests based on the things that they share with me, which is really nice," said a public relations specialist. "My oldest daughter, who went to Kenya, is now teaching environmental education. My son, who was in Asia, is now doing graduate work in wild land resource management. My younger daughter, whom I visited in Nepal, introduced me to trekking, and we did it for ten days last December. They share their interests and their lives with me, so I feel enlarged—not diminished— by their absence, by being able to make their interests my interests."

Some may say that sharing our children's lives represents yet another example of how we live *through* our offspring. I don't see learning from our sons and daughters as a vicarious experience but as a partnership of adults who respect and complement each other, just the way our friends introduce us to their interests. When Margot became a vegetarian, for example, she taught me a totally different way of eating. Alfalfa sprouts, tofu, and vegetables have expanded the standard fare at our house. Andrew, the computer maven, has tutored me to expand my computer skills and venture on-line. In these ways my children have broadened me and added texture to my life.

The new relationships we forge with our young adult sons and daughters can be richly rewarding—if we're willing to give up our old, worn-out roles and work at building new ties. These special relationships, in fact, can replace the full-time parenting jobs we are losing. So when our children leave home, we are not left with a void but with *the potential* for a mutually satisfying new connection.

BETWEEN HUSBANDS AND WIVES

Two out of the three dramatic divorce peaks occur at midlife: Between fifteen and eighteen years of marriage and again between twenty-five to twenty-eight years.[4]

Twelve percent of divorces occur after twenty years of marriage.[5]

These statistics are disturbing. Yet they make sense. When our last child leaves home, our focus becomes less family-oriented and more couple-centered. In raising our children, we often put the needs of our children or our family before our priorities as a couple. Even when we went out alone with our husbands, what did we talk about *a lot*? Our children. Although most of us recognized the importance of spending time alone as a couple, and many of us made continuous and conscious efforts to do so, we usually felt our children's omnipresence.

Now with our children launched, we look at our husbands and wonder: Is this the man with whom I want to spend the next thirty years of my life? Do we have a strong enough relationship to survive? And can we not merely survive but find true pleasure in the years ahead? These questions can be unsettling, yet exploring them is necessary to help us understand and reinvent our marriages without children at home.

Eileen O'Malley, a graphic designer, has asked herself these questions many times in the last three years since her son and daughter left for college. Married to Tom, an architect, for twenty-five years, Eileen has begun to acknowledge that Tom may be an alcoholic. Although many of their battles resulted from his drinking, she knows now that she played a part in perpetuating them. When Tom would come home drunk in the past, she would confront him and harangue him continuously so he couldn't sleep. Then she would be so upset that she couldn't fall asleep either. Last Friday night, she told me, she responded differently: "When he came home after drinking too much, I said, 'Tom, I don't have to stay here anymore. I am here because I want to be here now. I am not going to argue with you anymore.' And I went to sleep.

"There is nothing holding me here. I am making enough money that I can live on my own. If his drinking continues, I am leaving. I won't go through all that arguing again. I'm not going to spend days not talking to him because I am so mad at him. I won't do it."

Eileen admits now that she stayed with Tom because of their children for much of their marriage. They fought constantly: She didn't like his friends and thought he drank too much and didn't work hard enough. He felt she overindulged the kids and ran around too much. With their children gone, they realized that they do care about each other. Now they want to be together—for themselves. A small incident illustrates how their relationship has changed. When Tom had financial problems in his business and had to let his secretary go, Eileen offered to pitch in and answer the phones. He appreciated her loyalty. In the past, she had criticized him for not working hard enough; now she saw firsthand how industrious he was and how the shaky economy—not Tom's work habits—had affected their finances.

"We both want to be here now. It is a choice," Eileen says. "I thought we *were* together for the kids for a long time. Maybe I still might not want to spend the rest of my life with him, but we are getting along well now, we're more supportive of each other instead of fighting all the time, and it is comfortable, very comfortable."

Sometimes, though, when a child leaves home—particularly a child with significant emotional problems—a couple's equilibrium can be thrown off balance. Families often create child-centered triangles that serve the purpose of lowering the anxiety between the couple, according to psychologist Harriet Lerner. Forming triangles can cover up real relationship issues between husbands and wives by focusing intensely on the child and his or her problems. For example, if a teenage daughter has an eating disorder, her parents may be so consumed with helping her get better that their own issues go underground. On a deeper level, though, some family therapists believe that the daughter, known as the "designated patient," is acting out issues in the family by getting sick. Triangles are not necessarily wrong or bad but adaptive ways to manage anxiety.[6] With the difficult child out of the picture, however, marital issues emerge.

With few exceptions, all the women I interviewed found that the sheer relief of having the "problem" child out of the house superseded all other emotions. One woman with a particularly rebellious son talked of how liberated she felt now that she and her husband could go out for the evening and not worry about what their son was doing or whether they'd receive a call from the police.

My Turn

Most of their disagreements had centered on disciplining their son. With him out of the house, their fighting diminished, and they enjoyed each other more.

Couples who are disappointed in their children, critical of their current lifestyle choices, or struggling to accept their child's chronic emotional problems have a harder time putting their kids in the background—even with them out of the house. Yet these parents have a greater need to experience good times than couples whose children follow a more traditional path because the parents need relief. If they have not worked through their issues, they may still blame each other, disagree on how to handle the problem, or feel guilty about enjoying themselves while their child is suffering.

Whether our children were particularly challenging or not, their departure changes the dynamics at home. We must remember that our husbands, too, feel the loss of our children. Their reactions were as varied as the men themselves, according to their wives. Generally, our husbands were not as profoundly affected as we were, primarily because few of our husbands' identities were as closely allied with parenting as ours. Those husbands who missed their children most were the more involved parents. Men who had difficulty relating to their children as youngsters and now saw them as "people" felt the loss keenly too: They were just beginning to connect with their children in a meaningful way—then they leave.

Many women told me that their relationships with their husbands improved when their children left home, because their major disagreements had centered on how to manage the kids. Others said they got along better because their husbands felt more important now that they no longer had to share their wives with their children. "Good old Freud is alive and well," said a social worker, referring to the Oedipal conflict between fathers and their sons. "My husband has me all to himself now. It's that simple."

OLD ISSUES RESURFACE

Unresolved issues from early in our marriage often reemerge after our youngest child leaves home. Because we focus so much of our energy and attention on raising our children, our own issues as a couple may burrow underground for years, unless they are too blatant to be ignored. Couples like Eileen and Tom O'Malley, above, who stayed together for the children, must now confront their differences, whether long buried, just under the surface, or conspicuous. Otherwise, they face becoming a divorce statistic.

But every couple, no matter how happily married, has issues that need work. Without the distraction of children and constant activity, these concerns come to the fore. A personal experience confirmed this for me. When we were first married, I was aware that Dick and I had differing needs for closeness and distance. This difference created some rumbles in the early years of our marriage, but once the children arrived, we were so busy raising them, juggling work and family responsibilities, and trying to fit in a social life that the issue virtually disappeared.

About three months after Margot left for college, I started feeling confined. I had spent the first couple of months reveling in my freedom. Then I got tired of running around and just wanted to settle in. Before I realized it, we were back to our old routine: I was cooking every night, and we were eating at 6 p.m. I still went to meetings during the week but stopped making plans with friends, because I felt guilty about going out and leaving Dick home alone. I had plenty of time and freedom, yet I felt hemmed in and angry.

After stewing for a couple of weeks, I realized how I had created this situation and had myself to blame. I told Dick that I didn't want to eat so early every night. No problem. Then I told him I resented cooking every night and wanted him to share the cooking.

No problem. Eventually we got to the real issue: our differing needs for space, closeness, and variety. I needed to be out more and wanted to spend more time with my friends. Dick, on the other hand, was happy staying home and preferred being with me.

Then we negotiated ways for each of us to feel satisfied. Dick told me to feel free to go out when I wanted and to make plans with my friends. He said he was content for now and that when he got sick and tired of staying home, he'd make a change. I told him that I didn't want to be out every night, but I wanted to feel free to go out and not feel like I was abandoning him. We both agreed that Friday and Saturday nights would be our "date nights."

How had this issue evaporated for twenty years? Had it simmered beneath the surface, unbeknownst to us? Had one of us shelved it to the back burner? Neither of us consciously avoided it. So much of our energy had gone into tending to our kids that we had little left over for ourselves. Now that they were gone, we could concentrate on our relationship. We were alone again, just as in our pre-children phase, only now we had the time and the maturity to resolve issues that raised red flags for either of us. Once again, we could concentrate on our relationship.

NEW ISSUES EMERGE

Gray Hair. Crow's Feet. Thick Hips—physical signs of aging. We can't avoid them. We see them every morning in the mirror. They haunt us in our marriages, forcing us to face issues we never dreamt we'd face as a couple. Older couples worry about hearing loss and impotence—*not us*. Yet here we are.

Physical Aging/Psychological Ripples

We swore we'd never gain weight, but we feel fat. We vowed we'd never have a face-lift, but now we're considering it—maybe just a tuck under the chin. When we can't sleep at night, we wonder: Will we be able to hold on to our husbands as these physical signs of aging creep in? Does he need a younger woman to make him feel vital?

Theresa O'Hara, 55, worries constantly about these questions. She has been married almost thirty years, has launched three children, and now runs a bookkeeping business from her basement. A pretty woman with deep lines on her face, she fears that her husband, Tom, an executive, will leave her. "I know that I'm not going to grow old gracefully. My appearance is deteriorating. I feel insecure," she says. "Tom has just ordered a new car. You want to hear my philosophy on that? I'd rather he get the neatest, most exotic car that he could find than take a mistress.

"There's still the sense of insecurity: Why is he with me when there are so many younger women out there? You have to always make yourself necessary. After I cook dinner, I ask, 'Does it get me two more days?' It's a joke, but it's a fear too. 'Did you really like your dinner?' I feel a little bit reassured when he does."

Not all women feel so insecure in their midlife marriages, nor are they so dependent on their husband's approval. Theresa put extra energy into cooking dinners, hoping that the way to her husband's heart, after thirty years, was still through his stomach. Her solution seems like a simplistic response to a complicated situation.

Since many of us married men a few years our senior, we must also cope with the implications of our husbands' aging. Some of us have already faced our husbands' deaths. We are coping with their slowing down, their disabilities, and their vulnerabilities. Barbara James, who teaches fourth grade, spoke in great detail about how her relationship with her husband, Leon, changed after his heart attack at age 52. "When he was sick he was totally absorbed within himself. It was like having another child leaning on me. I felt unappreciated.

I didn't need, 'Oh, Darling, thank you so much,' but I did not need to be snapped at. Every problem he dumped on me. At one point, I must admit, I didn't know where to turn. I thought that this is supposed to be my turn, but he was dumping on me. My daughter had her own emotional problems, and my son was involved with his wife, so I had no one to turn to.

"The hardest part was that he became so internal. I am sitting there with this silent partner, and my husband used to be very gregarious. I would try to make conversation, but I'd get no response. I had to back off because I was so angry."

Barbara has every reason to be angry: This was not the man she had married nor the type of relationship she had anticipated at midlife. Leon had built every shelf in the house and loved to cook, dance, and socialize. Following his heart attack, he withdrew from her and from all of his activities. That was four years ago. Fortunately, in the last few months, Barbara says, Leon has regained much of his former vigor. Now they both look back and are able to laugh at how impossible he was to live with.

Not all couples are so lucky: Some must face permanent physical changes in a partner. One woman whose husband lost his hearing spoke of how frustrated and angry she becomes because she must constantly repeat her words. She knows his hearing will not improve; they will both have to accept his hearing loss and learn to communicate in less frustrating, more constructive ways.

Together but Out of Sync

Even if we and our husbands both enjoy good physical health, we may clash emotionally and psychologically. We feel energized, released from our caretaking responsibilities. We're invigorated, ready to use this time for self-discovery, personal growth, or career involvement. Our husbands, on the other hand, who have logged twenty-some years in the workforce, are ready to slow down or slack off. They want to relax and spend more time with us.

Our husbands may feel vulnerable when we start making changes in our lives. They worry: Will she outgrow me? And their unspoken fear, at 3 a.m., is: Will she leave me? When our husbands feel threatened they often react by trying to subvert our efforts to develop ourselves. In fact, an unpublished doctoral dissertation on women at midlife found that the largest deterrent to a woman's growth was her husband's objections.[7] My interviews bore this out: One woman told me that when she signed up to take a French course, her husband insisted on taking it with her. It was almost as though he was afraid to let her out of his sight. Another woman said her husband objected when she visited a friend overnight in a neighboring town. She went anyhow, despite twinges of guilt.

In a disconcerting study, researchers Margaret Fiske Lowenthal and Lawrence Weiss found that eighteen months after the youngest child left home, husbands and wives experienced similar high levels of mutuality and happiness, almost as though they experienced a second honeymoon. Five years later, however, the researchers found that the long-range goals of men and women were on a "collision course": Many women hoped to become committed to some activity or interest beyond the family, while their husbands hoped to be yet more pampered by their wives in order to ease them through another ten or fifteen years of boredom on jobs to which they had relatively little commitment and even less hope of changing.[8]

A sad prognosis. Our husbands are tired of working; they want to be pampered. But we're tired of giving; we need time to rejuvenate ourselves. What's a couple to do? Of course, we could live together and lead independent lives, but then why stay married? It takes work to revitalize our marriages, as we all know. Here's how one couple reconnected despite their differences.

Esther Prager yearned to travel since her kids were babies. Her husband, David, refused. They could afford to travel; he just didn't like leaving home. "I resented it for years," says Esther, "Now with the kids out of the house, I'm freer. I always ask him first, and if he doesn't want to go, I just go with my girlfriends. In the last two years, I've been to Europe twice without him.

"Now we're going to London for New Year's, and it's his idea. How about that? I didn't go without him to 'show' him, because if I did it to prove something to him, it wouldn't have worked," she says. "I basically learned if I want to do something and he doesn't, I can still do it. I'm making money now so in a lot of ways, we don't have an old-fashioned marriage. I think I'm becoming much more emotionally independent."

With her children out of the house, Esther had no reason not to travel. However, she could have sulked, withdrawn, or continued blaming her husband for not accompanying her. Instead, she took ownership of the problem and solved it herself. Eventually her husband joined her of his own accord. She handled the situation in a healthy way, taking care of her own needs without denigrating her husband or acting vindictively. She accepted their differences, as did he. In the long run, they grew closer as a couple.

Sexual Adjustments

We and our husbands can be at different places sexually too. Our middle-age husbands frequently begin to experience some loss of potency and a slowing down of their sexual reactions while we often feel freer and more responsive sexually without our kids at home. Our sexual assertiveness, however, can threaten our husbands if they feel insecure about their potency. We, on the other hand, may experience a loss of lubrication caused by hormonal changes that accompany menopause. This can make us avoid intercourse, because it can be uncomfortable or downright painful.

These differences are not insurmountable. First, it's helpful to understand just which sexual changes are a normal part of aging. Sometimes a very simple solution, such as using a lubricating jelly for vaginal dryness, can solve the problem. Generally, though, we need to talk honestly and openly about our individual needs: what's pleasurable and what's not; what we prefer, and what turns us off; how frequently we want sex, and what time of day we're most interested. If your husband is insecure about his sexuality, he needs reassurance not only in words, but in hugs and caresses.

Once these difficulties are resolved—and it may take months and require professional help—many couples find their sex lives improve without their children at home. No longer are we torn between our roles as mother and lover. It's easier to relax knowing our children won't pop in unannounced. We can also be more spontaneous and enjoy the moment—no matter what time of day or night. Having our children and their problems "out of sight, out of mind" frees us sexually too.

ENHANCING THE RELATIONSHIP

For husbands and wives who have successfully launched their children and negotiated satisfactorily their differing needs and priorities at midlife, this can be a time of deep intimacy and pleasure. Still, it takes work. It requires focusing on our marital relationships, making them a priority, then finding ways to enhance our lives as couples.

Susan Eisner, a part-time social worker, and her husband, Ben, a dentist, have always made their relationship a priority—even when raising their daughters, now 21 and 23. As far back as they can remember, they reserved a half day each week to "play," often going hiking or cross-country skiing or just "hanging out" together.

Still, they knew that when their younger daughter left for college, even *they* would need to focus on each other in a different way. At Ben's suggestion, they signed up for a course in Tantra, an Eastern spiritual sexual philosophy. "It gave us a totally new direction, a way of focusing on each other in a sexual way," said Susan. "It was a class about intimacy, connecting through our sexual energy. We had fun, and we could practice having a darn good time!" Through lectures, exercises, and practices, they learned how to create an effective environment and setting for intimacy.

Now they often hold Tantra evenings at home. They set aside an evening just for themselves, light candles to create a mood, and pleasure each other. "We are doing new and different things as a couple, and we're keeping our relationship vibrant and alive," said Susan. "Our relationship has changed. We have a greater respect for one another. We're closer than we've ever been. And logistically, we have the space and the opportunity to do it."

Other women told me that they have achieved greater intimacy with their husband—outside the bedroom. Anne Ross, a journalist married to Nick, a sociology professor, reflected on the differences in their early marriage and their relationship today, after almost twenty-seven years together. "If someone had asked me frankly who were the most important people in my life when I first married or even when I first had children, I would have said my kids first, my best friend next, and then Nick. I lived three blocks from my best friend, but I spoke to her more intimately than to Nick," she says.

"Now, there is no question in my mind that Nick is my best friend, and I think that is the reason why it has been so nice since the kids left. The focus is away from the kids. We never took a vacation away from the kids, and we didn't have baby-sitters that often. It was just not a big deal then. Now I feel like I am making up for that lost time.

"My time with Nick is just more fun. He can really make me laugh, and I can make him laugh just for no reason. We are very different people, but it surprises me how alike we often see the world or certain people or certain things. We are just in tune."

What did it take for Anne and Nick to become best friends and for Susan and Ben to become more intimate after their children left? Both partners wanted to improve their relationship. Many of us find that we're more "in tune" with our husbands because *they* are more interested in relationships now. Formerly they focused on making a living, and we were the relationship makers and healers. Now, as our husbands seek more balance at midlife, they want to spend more time with us and our families. As they take stock of what's important to them, they find that relationships do matter. And they're willing to work to make them better. This can work to our advantage: We can use our husbands' new interest in relationships to foster better marriages, as long as we keep the following in mind.

Set boundaries. Of course, we, too, want more intimate, closer relationships. But we also need to take better care of ourselves as women. That means we need to define our boundaries so that our individual needs do not get subsumed by the relationship. If you truly prefer to take a French class by yourself, you need to tell your husband. If you'd rather have lunch with a girlfriend on a Saturday than go hiking with him, he needs to know. Now, as always, open, clear communication is the key to enhancing our relationships.

Accentuate the positive. Our lives have changed: The kids are gone, we are getting older, our husbands are aging. These are all normal changes. Rather than yearning for the past or dwelling on the loss, work on ways to enrich your life as a couple now. Long-term relationships stay fresh when each partner brings something of his or her own, whether it's a new friend or a new interest or hobby. Finding new interests as a couple can also keep your marriage interesting. Maybe you can't go mountain climbing any more, but you can find other interests more suited to your current tastes, whether it's swing dancing, opera, or antiquing.

Most of our marriages undergo a transformation once our children leave home. We are looking for a way *through* this juncture—not out of our marriages. Our task now is to embrace our marriages as we refashion them to meet our needs. We still want that sense of belonging that our marriages give us, yet we also need to take care of our individual selves. With effort on our husband's part and our own, we can achieve a true, lasting partnership.

JUST FRIENDS

"What do you *talk* about?" Dick asks as I return from my morning walk with a close friend. "Our lives," I answer cryptically. And we do. We cover our feelings, our work, our kids, our husbands, our health, our aging—all at 7:30 a.m. When I have a pressing problem, I know I can count on her to listen to me, support me, and if necessary, problem solve. Most of the time, I just need her to let me talk. And when she needs to talk, I'm there for her. If both of our lives are going well, we may just chatter. But whether we talk about the worry that kept us up half the night or our reactions to daily headlines, these morning walks and talks have become vital to my well-being. When it rains several days in a row, or it's too cold to walk, it's not just the exercise I miss: I need my friendship fix.

I didn't always feel this way about my friendships. Although I always enjoyed spending time with my friends, work and family took precedence. Many of the women I interviewed, particularly those who are divorced and widowed, shared similar friendship histories: Working full-time and managing a household by themselves, there just wasn't time to talk on the phone or see friends. Their children ranked first; their friends would have to understand. Alma Washington, a grade school teacher, remembers having little time to breathe, let alone socialize, while she raised her daughter alone: "I was a single parent, a graduate student. I worked full-time as a teacher and went to school at night. I had a house and a short acre of land. Just trying to get the grass cut was a monumental task. Then Susie wanted dancing lessons, that kind of thing. I always had friends, but the things we did were centered around the children. I just couldn't hang out with the 'girls.' I had very few relationships with women."

But when her daughter left for college, Alma joined several women's groups and started traveling with her female friends. Last year she vacationed in Jamaica with her social club—three hundred women strong—and had a ball.

Research supports the fluctuating role that friendship plays in our lives. We all know how much friends matter to adolescent girls—how they talk on the phone for hours, how they leave their friend's house and call her the minute they walk in the door. In early adulthood, though, friendships take a back seat to forming romantic attachments, creating families, and launching careers, British scholar Terri Apter found. In fact, in her study, young adult women referred to friends less than half as frequently as girls and adolescents did. However, when she interviewed eighty midlife women, she found that they made nearly as many references to friendship as did adolescent girls.[9] Apter confirmed what most of us already know: Friendships matter again.

My Turn

When my children left home, I found that friends became more important to me and a more integral part of my life—in part because I had more time to spend with friends, in part because I enjoyed being with other women, and in part because they filled an urgent need for me. I felt more vulnerable: My role as a mother was changing, my relationship with my husband was shifting, my work—while engaging—did not fill the void as I had anticipated. I had often felt vulnerable in the past, but I had not turned to my friends when I hurt. For some reason, I needed to erect a front of being "together." Now I had moved beyond that: I *needed* to talk about my feelings and experiences and learn from my friends that I was not alone and that my experiences were normal. I found that the more I shared, the more my friends opened up to me. It seemed easier for me to talk candidly with my friends because by the time we had reached midlife, each of us had been through "something"—the illness or death of a parent, angst over a child, crisis in a marriage, loss of a spouse through divorce or death, or disillusionment in a career. At this point, none of us pretended to have perfect lives.

I was pleased to learn that Apter's research confirmed my experiences: She found that midlife women put less effort into hiding their vulnerability from friends than they did in adolescence or young adulthood; that they worried less about how they would be judged and assumed they'd be judged more favorably. And because they had fewer fears about being betrayed, they could reveal themselves without feeling exposed.[10]

Our friendships—particularly the long-term ones—also give us a sense of belonging and connection. They are "just like family" and indeed, with our children gone, we often celebrate the holidays and special occasions with them. My friends grounded me as I floundered, trying to make sense of the changes in my life without the children home. My friends experienced similar transitions, emotions, and upheavals, so we supported each other. It was comforting to know that we were all in this together—and we would all survive together.

Our friendships remind us of our own identity and can help us rediscover the parts of ourselves that make up our own unique "I."[11] Many of us submerged our "I" while we raised our children. But our friends, who relate to us as individuals playing many roles and wearing many hats, can reaffirm our identity as a person—funny, smart, irreverent—and support our affirming those hidden parts of ourselves.

Traditionally among married women, friendships have been relegated to second-class complements to the marital relationship. We all can remember incidents when our husbands called, and we cancelled plans with our friends. Research has blamed this on our culture's devaluing of "women's worlds" and our husbands' jealousy over conflicting commitments.[12] In midlife, however, as we reorder our priorities, we often find we prefer the company of our women friends to our husbands'. Even Erica Jong, who publicly chronicled her sexual escapades, recently wrote in her memoir about turning 50: "Are men really so interesting? To *themselves* they are. Yet, lately, I find women *far* more interesting. I have lived for men so much of my life that this comes as something of a shock to me. Have I been so bound by the conventions that I, supposed rebel, am as conventional as any woman of my time?"[13]

Many of the women I interviewed told me that spending time with their friends has become a priority, not just a fill-in when their husbands are unavailable. Why? Listen to a couple of the women I interviewed. Rachel, a 49-year-old married interior designer, told me, "I just love my girlfriends. I would rather take a vacation with them. We have the best time. We have fun—so much fun that we embarrass our children sometimes." When I asked Rachel what she and her friends did, she replied, "We go out to eat. We go to the movies. One of my friends likes to sing, and so we go to karaoke clubs and sing." These friends are doing nothing that unusual—yet they're having one terrific time together.

Other married women voiced similar sentiments. "I'm at a point in my life where I find my female friends infinitely more interesting. The men are okay, but once is enough," laughs a woman who just celebrated her twenty-fifth wedding anniversary. "I really enjoy being with women my own age. We don't *do* anything. Maybe we'll just go out for coffee or browse in a book store. And just talk."

Just talk. It doesn't sound like much. We're not *doing* anything. But talk holds women's friendships together. Through talking, we air our fears and our frustrations; we learn we are not alone and that our experiences are normal. Talking gives us the support we need to mobilize ourselves and the courage to move on with our lives. Whatever bumps we hit in the road ahead, we know our friends have either experienced them or if they haven't, will listen supportively to our travails.

As mothers of young adult children, we often wonder: What can I give my children now? When they were younger it was easier: We'd bake their favorite cookies, sew their Halloween costume, or help them with a school project. We had concrete ways to show our love. Now, we are at a different stage: We have moved beyond our daily caretaking roles. And our relationships have grown more complex.

The best gift we can give our children as young adults is to live our own lives fully. When we donate time to our favorite charity, when we run to a friend in need, when we save a weekend at the beach for our husbands—we show our sons and daughters that we value ourselves as women. Not through lecturing, not through preaching, but through living, we become models for our children. That's the only gift we can give them—and in turn, honor ourselves.

CHAPTER SIX

FREE AT LAST!

In Henrik Ibsen's classic play *A Doll's House*, Nora Helmer behaves like a "little lark" intent on pleasing her banker husband, Torvald. She fawns, she preens, she giggles. The drama of the play surrounds Nora's secret: She forged her deceased father's signature to obtain a loan without Torvald's knowledge so they could afford to spend a month in Italy while he recuperated from a life-threatening illness. When he learns what she has done, he calls her a criminal and a liar and forbids her to see their children. His real fear, however, is that public gossip about her deed will ruin his career. When the loan shark tears up the note, Torvald rejoices and welcomes Nora, his "frightened little song bird," back into his arms, under his protection. In a dramatic finale, Nora walks out on her husband and children because she realizes that she could not express her individuality in such an oppressive marriage.

When *A Doll's House* was produced in 1879, it caused a commotion: Managers of theaters in Scandinavia, Germany, and Italy urged Ibsen to write a new ending to the play that would assure its success with playgoers. He refused, saying that he wrote the whole play for the sake of the last scene.[1]

The central theme of *A Doll's House,* the emancipation of women, still resonates today. Nora left because her husband patronized her and treated her like a child: She wanted to be regarded as an equal. Women leave marriages in the 1990s for the same reasons. But whether or not we are currently married, many of us feel trapped by traditional caregiving and nurturing roles. Shouldering the major responsibility for child care, cooking, and housework keeps us overburdened more than 100 years after Ibsen wrote *A Doll's House.* Even with paying jobs, we carry the major responsibility for managing our households and our children's well-being. Of course, we chose to have children and had and continue to have deep emotions about mothering.

But now, with our sons and daughters out of the house, we get a taste of freedom, and many of us begin to recognize how limiting and restricting our lives have been. Yet *until this stage of our life arrives,* we didn't realize we felt so confined. Even the most previously contented among us seems to find that suddenly *now* she craves space, choice, and self-direction.

"When I was raising the kids, I didn't know any difference. This was my life," says Norma Block, a 54-year-old mother of two from Wilmington, Delaware, who devotes hundreds of hours each year to the local hospital antique show. "When I think back on it, I realize there was a part of me that felt really locked in here, especially all those years raising the boys. I could not get away. My parents had died. My husband's parents had died. There was nobody to leave the kids with. I was always busy with something: carpooling, school, my community obligations. My husband couldn't get out of work, so I had to be here. Once the kids were gone, though, I didn't have those responsibilities. I could start to think a little bit more about myself. Now I go to Philadelphia whenever I feel like it; I go to Florida to visit friends. *I just go.*"

Freed from the confines of caregiving, Norma Block travels when she pleases. Another woman, a management consultant, told me that for years she yearned for light and water, both symbols of freedom. When her children moved out, she painted her entire kitchen white; now she's trying to convince her husband to move near the ocean. A third woman, a teacher, bought a sailboat when her youngest child left for college.

In many ways, these women are sailing uncharted waters. For the first time in their lives—and in all our lives—we feel free to do as we please. Gone are the daily responsibilities, chores, and hassles with our children. What a relief! Without the structure of mothering to define our lives, though, identity questions resurface—even for those of us with jobs or careers. Now we wonder: Who am I without my children at home? What am I going to do for the rest of my life? Searching for answers, we begin an exploratory process: unearthing interests, hobbies, or ambitions put in storage while we actively parented, unleashing parts of our personalities held in check "for the sake of the children," following our bliss.

Such freedom can be exhilarating, but it can also be frightening. Not all of us welcome our liberation with open arms. We hold back because of our own personal anxieties or because of our trepidation about how our relationships will be affected. Yet I was struck by how many women, some of whom you'll meet later in this chapter, have successfully overcome their fears to embrace their freedom.

FREEDOM FROM . . .

When our children leave home, we feel liberated from the daily grind of churning out dinners, cleaning up clutter, gauging our teenagers' moods, refereeing sibling disputes, and enduring the arguments that inevitably accompany decision making with teens.

When I spoke with Pamela Johnson, a space planner from St. Louis, whose son Jim and daughter Carrie attend college in California, she minced no words in talking about how relieved she felt to be uninvolved in the daily ups and downs of her children's lives. "Carrie called the other day and was crying that she was 3 credits short and may have to go to summer school. I felt so bad for her, but I hung up, knowing her boyfriend would take care of her," said Pamela. "It was a wonderful feeling. Normally, when she was home, I would have to listen to it for days. I would foster it. I would talk about it.

"Then Jim called and told us he was going to drop out of school. He said he didn't know what he wants to do with his life. If he were home, that would have paralyzed me. I would have been devastated. But I remember thinking how well I took it. I was so removed from it physically—because he is in California—and mentally—because I think I finally separated from him—that I could say, 'This is your life, Jim.'"

She continued to reminisce. "When they were in high school, I was so 'into' every part of their lives. It is really liberating not to be anymore. I always felt that I had to be involved. Everything that was wrong, I had to fix. Now I know this is not good. The kids have to fix it themselves. I also feel like I don't have any control, yet I love it. I just love it. I'm such a control person and yet I feel very free now that I don't have to control their lives any more."

Giving up "fixing" and controlling everything in her children's lives has freed Pamela. With Carrie and Jim out of the house, Pamela has more time and energy, both physically and emotionally, to focus on herself and give her space-planning business the attention it needs. She has begun enlarging her offices and expanding her client base to include more geographically diverse businesses.

FREEDOM TO . . .

Once liberated from the daily burdens of caregiving, we face unlimited possibilities and overwhelming choices. One woman became so exhilarated by her freedom that she fantasized about leaving her family altogether, getting her own place, and starting over. "It was weird. I got a little selfish once the kids left," said Judy Kramer, a 45-year-old happily married woman with a son and daughter in college. "It was like I'd like to have my own place, a little town house where it's totally clean, and nobody can mess it up. I'd like my own car that none of them would junk up. I had all these kinds of thoughts and maybe . . ." she pauses and whispers, "I thought I might even like to date again. It was almost as if that life was finished, and I was going to move on and maybe even start again. That's kind of ridiculous, but those thoughts did go through my mind." It may sound ridiculous, but we've all had these thoughts. We've all had days when we just want to dash it all and hop an airplane or slip behind the wheel and keep driving.

But we don't. We stay and confront issues we have never faced before: How will I fill the hole, that emotional void, created by my children's departure? Who am I, apart from my history and the roles I have played? These identity questions plague all of us, whether we work outside the home or are homemakers. In fact, several research studies have shown that women gain their primary identity from their relationships, not from their work. Carol Gilligan, for example, found that even highly successful women describe themselves in the context of an important relationship, not in terms of their academic or professional standing.[2] Lillian Rubin, author of *Women of a Certain Age*, found that none of the 160 women she interviewed described herself in relation to her work, including those who held high-level professional jobs. No one said, "I'm an attorney" or "I'm a psychologist." Nor did anyone label herself as competent or capable—even when Rubin interviewed them at their workplace. Instead, they described themselves with such adjectives as "loving," "kind," and "committed to relationships."[3] Whether we hold jobs, pursue careers, or do volunteer work, most of us obtain our primary identity from our intimate relationships. No wonder we feel lost at sea when the character of one of our most absorbing, emotional roles and relationships drastically changes.

Even for those of us who thought we had resolved identity issues as adolescents or as college graduates, the questions resurface now. We are different people than we were twenty-some years ago. Motherhood has changed us; our life experiences have matured us. Because we recognize the finiteness of the time left to us, we want the next thirty years to be satisfying ones. Yes, some of us are content staying the course we chose at 22. But many of us want "more" than we've had up until now and certainly more than our mothers had.

Thinking back, I know that my mother's life changed very little after my sister and I left for college. Her daily routines continued to revolve around my father. She cooked every night, serving dinner at the same hour. They spent their weekends with their same friends, eating at the same restaurants, watching movies at the same theaters. I don't remember her making any new friends, discovering fresh interests, or unearthing buried passions.

Was she unhappy? I don't know. I do know, though, that she lived in the shadow of my father and of us, her daughters. Everyone else, including my father's extended family, came first. I have often wondered what she would have done or whom she might have become if she had experienced the cultural permission and freedom to claim, "It's my turn."

My mother's generation grew up and raised their families in different times and under different circumstances than our own. Like most of her contemporaries, she did not work outside the home. Their lives were more contained, their goals less lofty. They had far less mobility and seemed to have far fewer conflicts than we do today.

We can look to our mothers for models in aging gracefully, for lessons in handling disability and illness, and for ways to be loving grandmothers. No small feats these. But few of us can turn to our mothers as role models for how to live without children at home. Why? Because most of us feel entitled to fuller lives: We want more meaningful connections, work that gratifies us, passions that grab us, and communities that warm us.

My Turn

I certainly yearned for all of these. And I found, bit by bit, that I could get most of what I wanted if I was willing to risk, if I dared to experiment, and if only I would value what I already had. I don't have everything I want, but then, who does?

I discovered yoga after a series of trials and errors as I searched for ways to simplify my life and feel less stressed. First, I tried a few introductory sessions of transcendental meditation, but I couldn't relate to the people who ran the program; they seemed *too* calm and detached. Then I tried a yoga class in a tiny, cramped room in the basement of the Y. The physical surroundings were not conducive to relaxing. Finally, I stumbled upon a new yoga studio in the area: a spacious room bathed in white. I took a round of introductory sessions and felt like I had come home. Yoga gives me a physical, mental, and emotional release. After each practice, I feel centered and calm. The tougher (physically) the practice, the more relaxed and mellow I feel afterwards. I try to get to class twice a week, but if I can't, I practice on my own, even if it's only for 15 minutes a day.

Yoga satisfies me in a deep, fundamental way. It has become a passion, yet I haven't owned it as such until now. I know yoga will continue being an integral part of my life. I want to keep taking classes, learn more about the meaning behind the practice, meet other yogi, and perhaps even teach yoga one day.

Writing, too, is a passion—a longtime passion. Writing is such a part of me, so integral to my sense of self that I may not have fully appreciated how much it meant to me. Writing is grueling work, no question, but there's nothing I'd rather be doing. With only a few more chapters to write, I've begun thinking about what I'll do when I finish this book. Within 2 seconds, I know the answer: Find another writing project.

Recently my ardor for writing spilled into a new direction, one that brings me a different kind of satisfaction: I've started teaching a noncredit course at a nearby university on how to become a freelance writer. I don't teach the mechanics or the craft of writing but the nuts and bolts of freelancing: how to write for newspapers and magazines, get a book published, treat your work as a business, beat writer's block, and handle rejection. Teaching allows me to give back and share some of my knowledge to help others get started. I've always wanted a mentor, but for one reason or another, I never found one. Now *I* have an opportunity to mentor. It's gratifying when my students tell me I gave them the tools to pursue *their* passion or call me months after the class ended with news that they made their first sale.

I've always loved the drama and emotionality of black-and-white photos. In fact, several cityscapes I took over twenty-five years ago still hang on the walls near my office. For years, every time I'd walk past them, I'd think, "I really enjoyed taking pictures. I must get back to photography." But I never did. One thing or another always got in the way. Six months ago, I decided I'm going to do it *now*. I signed up for a photography class at the university. At first it felt awkward even holding a camera more complicated than a simple point-and-shoot. But as I took roll after roll for my class, I grew more comfortable with the camera, and my enthusiasm from my pre-children days returned.

I know now that writing, yoga, and photography will be an integral part of my life in some way in the years ahead. I don't know what form they'll take, whom I'll meet pursuing them, or what new insights or rewards they'll bring me—that's exciting too. And I'm sure I'll find other passions as long as I'm receptive to new experiences and people.

WHAT DID I PUT ON HOLD?

We've all put personal priorities on hold for our families. We table the master's degree. We forfeit a promotion because we'd have to travel. We give up a romantic getaway weekend for a family vacation. Sacrifice is not new for women: Our mothers did it, and so did their mothers. What's alarming to me, however, is that girls learn to sacrifice their selfhood at a very early age.

Between the ages of 8 and 11, several studies have shown, girls embody their essential selves: They're full of confidence, speak their minds, and flaunt their smarts.[4] But by the time they reach 15 or 16, they've submerged their own identity to please their parents, attract boys, and comply with the cultural expectations for females. They keep quiet in class, say "I don't know" when they do, and choose English and foreign languages over math and sciences, the tougher courses. Hoping to be popular with boys, girls often mask their ambitions or minimize their accomplishments. "I was not a great student in junior high school and high school," a social worker who considers reading her greatest joy told me. "I knew I was concerned about being popular, but I couldn't quite pull both off . . . I let the school work go."

Conforming to the impossible feminine ideals of being pleasing, passive, and submissive prevents young women from developing themselves fully as individuals. For many of us, this subverting of our essential selves continues well beyond adolescence, even after we marry and have children. How many of us value our husband's career over our own? Do all the housework *and* hold down full-time jobs? Put our career advancement or education on hold "until the children leave"?

No longer. It's our turn now. Now we can push ahead full throttle in our careers or stop procrastinating about getting a graduate degree. We've lost our excuse: The kids have left. It's time to take action. But has the workplace stood still waiting for us, or has it changed so much that we've become obsolete?

Much to my surprise, I found that corporate women who chose flexible work arrangements, including working reduced hours while raising their children, could get back on track once they were ready to take on a full load. "These women plateaued while working part-time or flextime," explains Marcia Brumit Kropf, Vice President for Research and Advisory Services at Catalyst, the New York-based research and advisory organization specializing in women and workplace issues. "They haven't missed a window of opportunity. They've just delayed it." A 1993 study by Catalyst of flexible work arrangements at seventy companies found that opportunities do exist to work flexibly, although these are primarily for women and are "not the norm." Many women don't feel comfortable taking them, believes Dr. Kropf, because they fear they'll be seen as uncommitted to their careers. Their fears are not unfounded, the study showed: While women worked at a reduced level, they felt resentment from their coworkers and had to continually "educate" them about their choices. Yet despite this, a number of women received promotions while working part-time. Once they moved back into full-time responsibilities, their colleagues accepted them, with no stigma or lingering resentment.

There were no corporate women in my study who chose to work part-time or flextime while raising their children, but this information can be helpful to younger women moving up. As I wrote in the introduction, it was very difficult finding corporate women whose children had been out of the house up to six years. The reason? Most women in corporate management of the age span of my study—from 45 to 60—either sacrificed children or marriage for their careers or postponed childbearing and have younger children. I spoke to a number of women who have their pulse on the corporate culture and they confirmed this finding, as did Dr. Kropf.

The same scenario is true in law. More typical is a Philadelphia attorney with whom I spoke. At 48, she ranks as the most senior woman in a firm of 150. Her oldest child is 13. At her firm, attorneys can work part time as associates. They remain on the partnership track while working part time, but generally it takes them longer to become a partner because they have not handled as many cases. As in corporations, once the attorneys come back full time, it's business as usual.

Although women are free to pursue graduate degrees once their children leave home, some who postponed getting a degree find they no longer want it. Janice Bloom told me that now that she *could* get her degree—she has the freedom, the time, and the finances—her priorities have changed. For years she didn't know what she wanted to do with her life. Married to an ad executive, Janice drifted into interior decorating after helping her friends decorate their homes and taught herself everything she knows. Today she does very well in her field and has an impressive list of clients, including some big-name commercial accounts. About five years ago, she realized she wanted to go to law school. But she couldn't afford tuition then because she and her husband were still paying for their kids' college educations. Janice talked about law school day and night for five years, planning to apply once her kids got their degrees.

Now the kids have graduated; she *could* go to law school. But she feels she's too old. "I just don't know if I have the stamina. It's a lot of work," she says with a sigh. "I'm interested in trial law, and that's very stressful. I don't want to be a tax attorney or do trusts. I want to be in court. All my friends say, 'You would be a fabulous lawyer. Go for it.' But you know what? It's too much work. I'm getting tired. I don't know if I really want to get involved in that."

Shifting career advancement or higher education to the front burner requires making specific, concrete moves: We apply for admission to a professional school, sign up for a course, put in more hours at the office. When we decide to resurrect buried parts of ourselves like Debra Benson did, however, it requires internal soul-searching—no quick moves or easy solutions. A 49-year-old teacher in the Minneapolis public schools, Debra considered herself a free spirit before Angela, now 22, was born. A "sixties person," she marched against the war in Vietnam and for the women's movement and dreamed of writing the great American novel. Angela's father, whom Debra met at a peace rally, took off for California to "find himself" when Angela was a year old; neither Angela nor Debra has seen him or heard from him since then.

"I never thought I'd settle down so early in my life. I was pretty rootless before," Debra explains. "As a single person, I could live on a fairly low income. When I had Angela, I had to put down roots. I still think every day of leaving Minneapolis. I started teaching because I had to find a way to tie me down so that I wouldn't take off and do something reckless." She feels that raising Angela inhibited her social life, curtailed her political activism, and prevented her from taking a leadership role in organizations.

Now that Angela has been out of the house for four years, has Debra recaptured her spontaneity? Not yet. Although she says she felt a great *sense* of freedom with Angela's leave-taking, Debra immediately enrolled in a graduate program as a way to keep her mind stimulated to combat the tedium of teaching.

"The truth is," Debra says, "there are two personalities here. There's Debra who imagines herself the free spirit and then there's Debra, the responsible educator. Sometimes in my life I go down both tracks. If I go to the free spirit side, I'd love to retire and take my pension and travel from ashram to ashram or from interesting spot to interesting spot. As the responsible educator, I'd like to start a good program at a university level or in a school and do the 50-year-old adult thing."

Resolving the conflicting parts of herself gets harder as she gets older. "As I approach 50, am I going to be a free spirit and give up my pension?" she questions. "I have twenty-four years in. There are advantages for every year that I hang on." Debra can find many reasons for holding on to the status quo since Angela has left home. "The bottom line," she says, "is a sense of inadequacy. I fear that I don't have the real resources, the skills, the personality to go out and take on more of the world. If I played in a larger arena, I might fail."

BARRIERS TO FREEDOM

Fears inhibit many of us, like Debra, from pursuing our dreams and savoring our freedom. Putting "me first" can feel frightening and lonely, particularly in a culture that accuses women of being selfish when we do so. Risking creates its own repercussions: We could fail, or worse yet, we could succeed; then what? What would success mean for us? How would it affect our relationships?

The prospect of freedom can be so intimidating for some women that they become paralyzed. Rather than forge ahead, they preserve the life they led when their children lived at home. Olympia Petronis, the woman from chapter four who had difficulty letting go of her sons, maintained the same daily schedule after they left for college. She still rarely ventures beyond the confines of job, church, and home. She says she's content with her life. While her inactivity makes sense in light of the cultural messages she received, not every woman within a particular ethnic group follows the prescribed course. Today many women who grew up in traditional homes have careers and interests of their own. What, then, might be holding Olympia back?

Like Debra, "the free spirit" restrained by her pension, Olympia may also fear failure. Such women typically fear being judged by others or by their own severe self-critic. They tend to be perfectionists who, when disappointed in their performance or accomplishment, think they have not only failed the task but have failed as people. They view their ability or their performance as a determination of their self-worth. An outstanding performance signifies that they're an outstanding person; a mediocre performance means they're a mediocre person.[5] Because they fear they can never meet their own unusually high standards, they *plan* to take risks—but procrastinate endlessly. "I'll go back to school when the kids go to college," one woman says. But when the children leave, she has another excuse: "I can't go back yet. Mother/husband/ children still need me." Outwardly, such people may not seem competitive or perfectionistic because they lead such settled lives. Their fear of failure prevents them from acting on their competitive instincts.

We also fear success, a concept that came into public consciousness in the early 1970s when the popular press picked up psychologist Matina Horner's doctoral dissertation on the subject. In brief, her theory stated that success requires achievement, which necessitates competition. Since competition is a sublimated form of aggression and society disapproves of aggression for women, success is also negatively sanctioned as unfeminine. The conflict between being successful and being feminine creates anxiety in some women and causes them to avoid situations in which they could succeed.[6]

My Turn

While Horner's work pertained solely to women, many theories have offered explanations for why both men and women fear success. In almost every culture, certain sayings capture a universal superstition about the wheel of fortune: that the higher an individual rises, the lower he or she will fall. The ancient Chinese philosopher Lao-tzu said: "Failure is the foundation of success; success the lurking-place of failure." When Saul Bellow accepted the Nobel Prize in literature, he quoted the Bible: "Woe unto you, when all men shall speak well of you!"[7] When Jews praise someone, they often follow it with the Yiddish word "kenehore," literally meaning "against the evil eye." It's like saying, "Knock wood." In other words: don't tempt the gods or make them jealous.

Just what might happen if everything goes *too* well, if we become *too* successful? *We just don't know*—that's part of our apprehension. We fear reprisals if we surpass our parents, say the Freudians. There's an element of truth in that for most of us. We may also fear repercussions in our immediate family. How will our success affect our husbands—if we earn more money than they, gain more status, achieve greater fame, or do greater good? What about our children: Will they see us as exemplary role models, or will our success intimidate them because they think they can never live up to our achievements? And will our success distance us from our friends, create jealousies, or bring forth a round of applause?

Indeed, this barrier—anxiety about repercussions in our important relationships—often prevents us from embracing our freedom. While many of our husbands give lip service to our "doing our own thing," they often don't want anything to change at home. "My husband will ask me, 'Did I ever keep you from doing whatever you want?'" recalled Norma Block, who opened this chapter. "At the same time, when I say, 'I'm going to Philadelphia tomorrow,' he'll respond, 'Why do you have to go?' Then I get these little guilts. But if I really want to do something, I do."

In addition, men are often at a different stage of their lives than we when our youngest child leaves home, as I explained in the last chapter. Finally free, we want to use this time for self-discovery, mastery, and self-fulfillment. We are often just coming into our own, particularly in our careers, while our husbands, who have spent twenty-five-odd years in the workforce, may be ready to slow down. On the one hand, they're genuinely happy that we've made new discoveries. On the other, they want us to be there for them, just like we've always been.

With these barriers to freedom in mind, imagine that Olympia Petronis decided to go to law school after her sons left home. How might this play out in her family? Her husband might tell her that it was a wonderful idea but still expect her to make dinner every night, take his shirts to the laundry, and do the wash. He may get home earlier from work than she and read the newspaper, waiting for her to start dinner. If she had to do homework on the weekends, he may tell her he understands yet interrupt her with innocuous questions. She might also receive subtle criticism from her mother, who never went beyond high school, with such comments as "Why can't you just take it easy now?" or "Are you sure you're not neglecting your husband?" After a year and a half of law school, she may decide to drop out, saying, "It just wasn't worth the hassle."

If, however, Olympia had persisted and graduated, she may have had to cope with her guilt about holding a more prestigious position than her husband, gaining more status in the community, and possibly earning more money. If most of her friends had jobs—not careers—and their lives still centered on the home, she may have felt isolated and alone. A possibility exists, too, that if she asserted herself and became more powerful, her husband might feel more threatened. They might argue more and possibly divorce.

On the other hand, if she developed a strong support system of friends in law school, particularly women who went back to school later in life, she could flourish. If her husband saw a happier, more satisfied wife and supported her move to become more competent and capable, they might well build a far richer marriage as two individuals who bring their strengths and talents together at midlife after the children leave home.

Such is the nature of risk. We can't fathom how it will affect our lives or our relationships, but unless we chance it, we will never experience the opportunity that lies in the unknown.

JUST DO IT

We all feel ambivalent to varying degrees when faced with new opportunities: We feel torn between the safety and comfort of the known and the lure of the unknown. What enables some of us to move on with our lives while others stay put, lulled by the complacency of the familiar?

We all feel fear. Women who take risks move ahead in spite of it. We head for a job interview with our heart pounding, *but we still go*. We chair an annual benefit with shaking knees, *but we still go*. We join Toastmasters International with sweaty palms and a dry mouth, *but we still go*. We've learned that fear will accompany us as long as we continue to grow. If we wait until we're no longer afraid, we'll stay put. We take risks despite the fear.

We can lessen the fear, however. How? By doing what we fear, again and again. I know from experience that this method works. I've always been frightened of public speaking and avoided any situation in which I'd need to speak before a large group. But when my book about women and mentoring came out, I wanted to promote it. I felt anxious: Would I go blank? Would I make a fool of myself in front of an audience? From researching and writing the book, I became zealous about women's need for mentors and believed I had important information to impart that could help women advance. My desire to share what I knew and promote the book propelled me to give speeches and workshops—despite my fear. For my first few speeches, I typed out the entire speech verbatim—more than twenty pages triple spaced in eighteen-point type. I practiced so many times that I knew it cold, yet I needed my crib notes as a security blanket. Every time I stood in front of an audience, I quaked; but with each presentation, I became a bit more relaxed and my confidence grew a little.

With each presentation, I became more comfortable talking about my material and more assured in front of a group. Eventually I was able to give a presentation from a single note card. My confidence as a speaker grew from the actual speaking. Only through *doing*—giving speech after speech—did I feel better. I didn't wait *until* I felt better about public speaking to do it, because I'm sure I would have never felt good enough.

I found that as I told people about my apprehensions about public speaking, they told me stories of their own fears and how they conquered them. Yet somehow we think that only we are afraid of new challenges. *Everyone* seems more confident, we think. *Everyone* else is branching out into new areas. Everyone may appear this way, but that doesn't mean that they don't have anxieties too. I realized that not only did I have fears when I was on unfamiliar territory, but so did everyone else.

What makes it worth going through all this discomfort to risk something new? Why not just go on living the life we led when the children were home? "Pushing through fear is less frightening than living with the underlying fear that comes from a feeling of helplessness," writes psychologist Susan Jeffers in her book *Feel the Fear and Do It Anyway*. No matter how secure we feel in the cocoon we have built for ourselves, we live, consciously or unconsciously, with a dread that the day of reckoning will eventually come, says Jeffers. The wheel of fortune resurfaces again. People who refuse to take risks live with an anxiety, she believes, that creates more pain than they would feel if they took the risks necessary to make them feel less helpless. Although these feelings are unconscious for most of us,[8] you'll hear Sarah Milton talk about this very terror later in this chapter.

On a conscious level, other factors motivate us to move ahead despite our ambivalence. With our children gone, we've begun to recognize that we won't live forever. We've started counting time in terms of how much is left. We don't want to have regrets when we reach 65 that we *should* have gone back to school, we *could* have done more for the fight against AIDS, or we *wished* we had moved closer to our grandchildren. Now is the time to do "it."

We are sick and tired of doing for others. "I want to do something for me, something that will make a difference in my life or have the choice—not the obligation—to do for someone else," I heard again and again. Women's aspirations were not always monumental or expensive to accomplish. Achieving even the simplest of dreams can be gratifying. "The two things I always wanted to do was sculpt and go on an archaeological dig," recalled a bookkeeper who singlehandedly raised two sons. "When the boys left, I took classes at the local art center and sculpted my first piece. The instructor asked me, 'Are you sure you never sculpted before?' The clay was so central to me and so sensuous, I could close my eyes, and it was like I had done it before. It was just fantastic! I never did get on the archaeological dig—it was just too expensive. But that's okay." This kind of enthusiasm can overpower women's fears and propel them to move forward—despite their apprehensions.

Support, too, helps us plunge ahead. We need each other, our peers, to model how to live our lives after our sons and daughters leave home. Particularly as our roles change and we age, we need our contemporaries to validate our experiences and encourage new ventures. "We need to look at multiple lives to test and shape our own," writes Mary Catherine Bateson, daughter of anthropologists Margaret Mead and Gregory Bateson. "Growing up with two talented and very different parents, I have never looked for single role models. I believe in the need for multiple models, so that it is possible to weave something new from many different threads."[9]

Few people make "it"—whatever their "it" is—alone. The support they receive from others empowers them. Consider the power of Alcoholics Anonymous groups to enable people to stay sober. Look at the preliminary evidence on breast-cancer patients that suggests that those who take part in support groups have a better survival rate.[10] The acknowledgments at the beginning of any book, including mine, attest to the wide range of support an author needs to write a book—alone. Our relationships with our peers—the ones you know personally and the ones you'll meet in this chapter—can inspire us to embrace this opportunity now.

BREAKING THROUGH

The women whose stories you are about to read will not turn you green with envy. I chose these women *not* because they had all the answers, *not* because risking came easy for them, *not* because their lives have been fairy-tale perfect. Far from it. I selected them precisely because their lives seemed so normal, so ordinary. They could be your neighbors or friends. The women all work and have worked for years, but motherhood grabbed their heartstrings. They had far less support than many of us do. Sarah Milton is a widow; Mary Ann Simons, a divorcee; and Martha Ehrlich, a married woman whose husband took a dim view of her living her dream. Yet these women didn't blame themselves, nor did they act like victims or throw up their hands and give up. They all found the support they needed to forge ahead.

When their children left home, they faced the same identity questions we all face. They had the same fears about moving ahead, the same trepidations. They did not all make major transformations. But the shifts they made were significant for them, giving them a better quality of life and a more satisfied feeling when they woke up each morning.

I chose to profile these women because I could identify with their lives and their struggles. Listening to their stories made me feel more appreciative of the support I have, more accepting of my progress, and more optimistic for all of us. They heartened me with their persistence and their determination to press on, no matter what. I chose to profile them precisely because they made me believe that if *they* could move forward with all their baggage, we all could.

Each of these women, of course, has her own unique story to tell. In each, I think you will find something to give you inspiration and support to encourage you to take your turn.

Sarah Milton: Unearthing Her Passion

Sarah Milton has always danced. She took ballet lessons as a child, explored tai chi in college and later taught it, and took modern dance lessons while raising her daughter. A psychologist in private practice, she'd often squeeze in a dance class during breaks in her day. But she always danced within the confines of conventionality: a teacher or a classroom kept her safe.

Dance mattered to Sarah, but being a wife and mother came first, even before her psychology practice. Basically, she led a conventional life: raised her daughter by the book, followed the rules. Two years before her daughter left for college, her husband was diagnosed with liver cancer. He died within a year, despite six grueling months of radiation and chemotherapy. A widow at 45, Sarah savored the eighteen months alone with her daughter before she packed her duffles, stereo, and books into her van and drove her to college, four hours away. After a teary good-bye, Sarah returned to her huge, empty Victorian house in the Minneapolis suburbs.

I met Sarah four years later. She described how her budding confidence has enabled her to grow stronger year by year despite grieving her losses and feeling completely alone. "I just finished studying for the licensing exam in psychology. That license hung over me for the last eight or nine years, and I know if my husband were still alive and my daughter still at home, I probably wouldn't have done it," Sarah admits. "It's just too time-consuming, too draining. But having done it—the pure rigor of it, the constant studying for three months—I realize it was an extraordinary thing. It makes me feel much more secure inside myself. The simple discipline of it gave me a whole new feeling about myself: one of pride and satisfaction.

"I have a much better sense of my own self-worth—more so than other things I've done with my life, including being a mother or a wife. Being a mother and a wife, you're very dependent on other people. It's a very fragile thing. Don't get me wrong: I would never give it up. But now, it doesn't have the same solidity to me that I find in just trusting myself. Being a mother is still the single most important thing, but that doesn't mean that's what makes me feel best about myself or what makes me feel strong."

As her self-assurance grew, Sarah began to take risks she never dreamed that she, always the straight, by-the-book one, would take. Recently she *danced* and chanted the twenty-third psalm at a friend's son's Bar Mitzvah—really a piece of performance art—in front of 100 people. Afterwards, people came up to her and told her how she touched them. She herself was moved: "It was very satisfying," she said, smiling broadly. "Every time I step out and every time I do another project or complete something, it solidifies something in me that is wonderful. It empowers me to do more."

She reflects on how different this feels, compared to how she felt in the past: "All the years I was married, I had enormous support—financial support, emotional support, every kind of support—and I was always terrified. Deep down inside, I was terrified. I didn't look like it or act like it, but inside, I wasn't really sure I could take care of myself. And now that I really have to take care of myself and have been for the last several years, I'm no longer scared."

With growing inner strength, Sarah has begun to take risks in a more personal way, by exploring dance through a whole new medium. Two winters ago she traveled to the Caribbean Islands and fell in love with the music and the dance. Caribbean dance became her passion, one edged with fear. "This dance is very, very sexual. It touches something in me that feels closer to some fundamental part of me. It's slightly touched with danger, and that's part of what makes it exciting too.

"Now I'm doing a lot of island music here at home in a variety of places. I'm going to night clubs and dancing. I try to go with a girlfriend, and I make sure that both of us leave together, so I try to put some safety between me and that world. But while I'm there I feel absolutely transported. *Just transported.* I watch myself move through my own inhibition and fear, which is a lot of what night life is about for me, and just let myself go.

"I go scared every time. But it's a kind of scare, a kind of fear that I'm conscious of and I'm playing and working with. I want to manage it. I use all my senses. Some men I just dance with once, and I don't want anything to do with them. Occasionally there's a man that I want to stay and dance with. It's physically the closest thing I can do to be sexual but not have sex. That's very enlivening to me."

Sarah has unearthed a gutsy spirit that's been hidden for years. She used to think she had to go away physically to have an adventure. Now, she's learned she can take risks, somewhat calculated and careful, within minutes of home. She tries not to put herself in physical danger, but living on the edge excites her. "I never went to clubs. When I was in college I didn't go to fraternity parties. I was very serious, I studied a lot," she recalls. "The fact that I'm starting to have a night life feels filled with danger and mystery and all kinds of things that I never did."

As Sarah revels in her newfound audacity, she tries to assimilate who she is now. What she's learned about herself in the last few years didn't jibe with her old sense of self, so she expanded her vision to encompass her new identity without giving up the old, familiar parts she loves so well: "It surprises me that the same person who enjoys making Sabbath dinners and Passover Seders can go and stay out in a club until 4:00 in the morning. That delights me!"

Mary Ann Simons: Creating a New Life

"I always had my own identity and interests even though it was very clear to me that my family always came first," Mary Ann Simons insists, as though she's trying to convince herself. She is 53 and the mother of three daughters in their twenties. She has a Ph.D. in biology but worked in her husband Len's accounting office for ten years before her daughters left for college because he needed someone to do marketing and public relations. She says she didn't mind at the time because she could come and go as she pleased. But with Len logging 12-hour days in his business, all the chores fell on Mary Ann's shoulders. The three girls had braces; that meant countless trips to the orthodontist. One took gymnastics; another, tennis; the third, soccer—more carpools.

Within a year after her youngest daughter left for college, Mary Ann's husband walked out, which meant she also lost her job. "When Stacey left, Len and I confronted some of the things we had never faced before. I don't know if it was a midlife thing with Len, and he would have gone through it anyway," she says wistfully. "But, I must say that our separation was facilitated by our children leaving. He was back and forth four times during that two and a half years. Finally, I said, 'Enough.' He's been out since."

Today Mary Ann often looks back at those years and tries to sort out her own emotions. She's not sure exactly which emotions are a function of her children leaving and which are a result of her being single. Nonetheless, she says, "I had to reconstruct a life for myself: a whole new life that enabled me to tap into what my basic interests were, to what I cared about, and to my values. I really had to decide how I want to live the rest of my life—not just during this transition period. It was a very difficult process."

In essence, Mary Ann sought a whole transformation: She lost her husband, her daughters, and her job in her husband's office in one fell swoop. Not one to feel sorry for herself, she picked herself up and called a career counseling firm, believing that if she concentrated on the work piece first, other things would fall into place. A counselor there helped her develop a résumé. She looked at options in the pharmaceutical industry because of her Ph.D., considered teaching, and explored community development and the affordable housing cause, two areas she cared about.

Mary Ann followed the counselor's advice to the letter: She set up information interviews and networked constantly. But she lacked confidence because she had been sheltered in her husband's office for ten years. Plus, she didn't know what she wanted to do or whether she had any marketable talents. She recalls how insecure she felt: "This was a very difficult, unsure time for me. People think that I am very confident, but I did not feel confident at all. I felt very self-conscious and shy and defensive.

"If you've been the wife and the mother for all these years, especially if you have been nurturing and giving and have always kind of compromised your own self for someone else's agenda, then you're not sure at this point where you fit in. You are not sure what feels good. You're not sure where you want to be. You're not even sure what's right for you, unless you have been very focused. Part of this process is just saying, 'I could do this' or 'I could go here.' You learn what feels right, whom you feel comfortable with, where you want to spend your time. It was not easy, but the more you talk to people, the more you realize that they are really interested in telling you what they do. In the process of these interviews, I clarified my needs and saw where jobs were available."

Mary Ann learned not to approach large companies because they wouldn't take a woman over 50. What a blow! That information flattened her for two days. Then she reframed her search. "I needed to find someone who appreciated me as kind of an eclectic, renaissance person," she said, drawing on her strengths.

When she wasn't networking and interviewing, she volunteered at a local shelter for battered women. "I needed something to fill my life and make me feel like I was doing something that I cared about while I looked for a job," Mary Ann says. There she met

Sarah, her current boss, also volunteering. Sarah was looking for someone to run the public affairs program at the bookstore she manages, and the job met Mary Ann's needs perfectly. "It was kind of serendipity," she says, thrilled.

The rest of her life did not fall into place so easily. She dates some, but she spends most of her time with women. She says, "I go places that interest me, and if I meet men, fine." She went cycling for a weekend in the mountains with no other motive than biking on a lovely fall weekend and met a man who has turned into a good friend.

As a pragmatist, she tries to prepare herself for her future, but the reality is hard to take: "I know I face the prospect of being a single woman for the rest of my life. I also know that my children will probably not settle near me, so I need to develop my life as if that would be the case." That's a tough realization for anyone.

Mary Ann tries not to dwell on her aloneness. She volunteers for Sierra Club inner-city outings and takes courses at the university. Still, she admits, "There is pain to being alone. I know this is also the time of greatest opportunity—if I can embrace it and not let the lack of resolution in my life and the lack of security overwhelm me," she says, again trying to convince herself. "For those of us who were raised to have lives that were more or less constant, the lack of clarity isn't particularly easy to handle, or maybe that's just my personality—I was trained as a scientist. I work real hard to just accept and almost embrace the open-endedness of it: not to know exactly where I am going and how it is all going to work out."

Martha Ehrlich: Chasing Her Dream

Ever since she was a young child, Martha Ehrlich, a teacher from Janesville, Wisconsin, yearned to sail. Each summer her family rented a cabin in northern Wisconsin along Lake Michigan, but because her father was afraid of the water, they never set foot in a boat. She loved to watch the sailboats gliding by on the lake and dreamed of one day sailing herself. But because her husband Jim, also a teacher, was a landlubber and her children Sam and Susan had no interest in sailing, she never pursued it.

About five years ago, the summer after Susan left for college on the West Coast, Martha felt particularly bereft and rootless. She missed Susan: Summer had been their time to jog together. Cleaning out drawers one rainy Sunday, she found photographs from her childhood summers at the lake, which started her thinking: Why not start sailing now? The kids are gone, Jim is busy. This is my time.

Martha took sailing lessons and began sailing with a colleague who owned a sailboat, on Lake Mendota in Madison, an hour and a half from home. The following summer she bought a 17-foot sailboat, much to Jim's—and her own—surprise.

"I found it sort of took me aback. I never thought of myself as somebody who *wasn't* relatively liberated. I pretty much took care of my needs. But until I decided to buy the boat, I never realized how much my life, and especially our weekends, focused on what other people wanted to do: Jim's golf game, the kids' activities when they were at home. Doing something like sailing, which is a very male-dominated sport, was a little shock to me. I came to the recognition that I wasn't going to have the support of anyone in my family but that this was something that I wanted to do anyway. This was really for me: I wanted this, and I realized that I *could* have it, even if Jim didn't want it."

It wasn't that Jim opposed her buying the boat; he understood she needed to do something for herself. But he refused to have anything to do with sailing. "Something different took place in our relationship," recalls Martha. "I think he felt left out."

My Turn

Shortly after she bought the boat, she got an offer to teach at a great school in Madison, with a huge salary increase. She took the job, but it meant she had to commute 3 hours every day. "I was totally exhausted. I talked about getting a house in Madison, but Jim was still teaching in Janesville and didn't like Madison. He didn't encourage me at all. He made it so hard for me."

Every night Martha would come home and replay the same tapes in her head: Should I quit? Is the commute worth it? Why am I killing myself? A turning point came one night when she was talking on the phone with Donna, a close friend. Martha remembers the conversation well: "I was lamenting, 'What should I do? I'm exhausted. I can't keep commuting like this. Should I get a new job? I need to talk to a therapist to work this out.' Donna screamed at me, 'Are you crazy? You don't need a therapist. You need a house! Here's what you're going to do: You are going to start looking in Madison. I'm going to call you every week, and each time we talk, you'll tell me what you've done to find a place.' "

This pep talk encouraged Martha and gave her the kick in the pants she needed. She started looking for a house in Madison in earnest. Donna checked in every week, bolstering her to keep searching. "My problem was I was looking for the perfect place, a house that Jim and the kids would like, but I couldn't afford most of those," Martha recalls. Again Donna helped her set her priorities straight: "She said I should just get a place that I liked, for myself. She really pushed me. And she was right."

Martha found a house that suited her, just a block from the lake, and rented it for a year. In the beginning Jim rejected the whole set-up and had no enthusiasm about going to Madison. "He didn't like the house, he didn't want any social obligations there, nothing. The kids didn't want to come when they were on break," Martha remembers, still pained at the conflict. "It was a very difficult time for me. The whole thing had so many implications. It put such a strain on our marriage that the whole idea of enjoying it was threatening in a way."

But Martha stood her ground: She enjoyed her new job, she liked being near the lake so she could sail on a whim, and she started making new friends there. Jim continued to come to Madison, grudgingly. But slowly, over a period of months, the experience of being there brought a turnabout for Jim. Once he stopped fighting it, he enjoyed having a second house more than he thought. They made friends as a couple there, and he found he liked being able to walk along the shoreline. That made it possible for Martha to continue working in Madison. The following year she bought a small house.

"Today Jim loves getting away to our house on the lake on weekends and enjoys socializing with our friends there. Now that we own a house and I've fixed it up, the kids think it's great too," says a relieved and relaxed Martha. "I feel very fortunate. I got up this morning and walked for an hour along the lake before going to work. I treasured that walk: It was so beautiful, the lake was so pristine, not a soul around. It made me feel very much alive."

CHAPTER SEVEN

SEIZING
YOUR
TURN

If this book has revealed one
central truth, it's that our children's departure from home is a
catalyst for change. Because
they've been so central to our
existence, their leave-taking sends
ripples reverberating through our
relationships, our work, our identities, our very lives. No doubt in
reading this book you too have
wondered many times, "Who am
I now?" and "What am *I* going to
do with the rest of my life?"

MY TURN

Now is the time to find out. It's your turn to take charge, to seize this opportunity for your own growth and development. Rather than sitting passively on the sidelines and waiting for something to happen, *you* can make it happen—by seeking challenges and initiating change.

No question, change is a risk and can be unsettling. If you wait until you feel totally comfortable taking action, however, you may never do it. You need to take risks despite your fears, keeping in mind that everyone has trepidations about undertaking new endeavors and breaking out of old patterns. When journalist Tracy Johnston experienced hot flashes for the first time while on a rafting expedition down the Boh, the wildest river in Borneo, she knew the nature of risk would change for her at midlife. In her memoir, she writes, "If I wanted to define myself by facing challenges, I had better stop making them physical. I could take on spiritual challenges, intellectual challenges, emotional challenges—but how, and where, and which ones? The thought loomed up more monstrous, even, than another set of rapids.

"It did occur to me that there was something about the moments of happiness and contentment I was feeling on the Boh that might be key. If I was going to reinvent myself, turn menopause into some sort of rite of passage, I would have to look inward."[1]

Tracy Johnston took physical risks all her life; she needed to "look inward" for a different kind of risk as she aged. If you led a more sedentary life until now, consider seeking more physical risks. One woman told me she pushed herself to take long-distance bicycle rides, 60 to 70 miles at one time, so she could stay in shape as she got older. Another used her fiftieth birthday as the trigger for losing weight. "Ever since I was 10 years old, I worried about weight. I felt fat, obsessed about it every day," she said. "I decided that my gift to myself would be that I'd try to get my weight under control and not live the next forty years obsessed with weight." She has lost 45 pounds so far, exercises every day, and has eliminated fat from her diet. She concludes, "I did all these boring, boring things, but it's been wonderful. It was scary for me: I didn't know how I'd feel as a slimmer woman. But I just feel so much better and much more confident."

Yes, risking inspires confidence. Even if you don't achieve the results you hoped for, you'll feel better for summoning the courage to try something new. In this chapter, you'll learn specific strategies to help you begin thinking about yourself and your life in a different light—in a way that will enable *you* to make the changes you want, recognizing and overcoming some of the roadblocks that may temporarily thwart you along the way. *You* will determine what kind of shifts you feel comfortable making and when *you* are ready to make them. Consider beginning this process *now*, whether your kids are still in high school, have just left for college, or have been out of the house for years. It's not too late.

CONSIDER YOURSELF NUMBER ONE

When was the last time you did something *you* truly enjoyed— not something that pleased your husband or your children, but something that gave you pure pleasure? Search back for weeks, months, or even years if you have to. Maybe your needs have been on the back burner for so long that you're not even sure what you like anymore!

"We need to really learn to stop focusing all of our energies and emotions on our husband's work and on what our kids are doing," said Judy Kramer, the homemaker who bought a frozen yogurt franchise after her children left for college. "So much of our energy goes into that, and we don't focus enough on making ourselves happy. That's a big, big issue for a lot of women: What is it *I* want? What do *I* want to do with the rest of my life?"

She's right. We've spent most of our lives pleasing others: first our parents, then our teachers, and later our husbands and children. Society has convinced us that we're selfish if we think of ourselves before caring for others. And after years of deferring to family, it can be difficult to make our needs and desires a priority. Once child-free, how do you suddenly cast off the societal and parental dictums that you've carried for forty or fifty years? And how do you discard the guilt for not bowing to these "shoulds"?

Becoming aware of your conflicting feelings is the first step toward resolving them. If you are not ready to shed the "shoulds"—and many women move slowly in this area—at least try to recognize when you are acting to please somebody else. That awareness will eventually lead you to change your actions.

To begin making yourself a priority, consider the following questions: In what ways do I need to take better care of myself? Think about what would make you feel better—physically, mentally, and emotionally. Do you want to begin exercising on a regular basis or eat more healthily? Do you wish to spend more time with your friends, or do you crave more time alone to read or garden or meditate? Would you like to give up a stressful job to find more rewarding work? Or maybe take on more challenges at work?

Making your own needs and desires a priority shows you and your family that you value yourself. You'll feel good that you've done something that you truly enjoy—just for you. You'll also experience an added benefit: You will *feel* less invisible. And in fact, you will be less invisible because your words and deeds will make a statement that honors your wants and needs. Every change, no matter how small, will make you feel proud of yourself and will empower you to do more.

WHO AM I NOW?

Now you have the time, energy, and desire to pursue your passions, but where do you begin and how do you find them? Are you someone who wants to do *everything* now that you're child-free, or do you feel like you're floundering, unable to focus wholeheartedly on *anything* that holds your interest? Or maybe you're somewhere in the middle: You have an inkling of a direction you might take, but you still feel unsure of whether you're ready to plunge into one particular activity.

No matter where you see yourself, this is a good time to take a self-inventory. If you really think about these questions and don't just gloss over them, you will give yourself an opportunity to learn a lot about yourself, your pleasures, and your cravings. Take this inventory seriously, and you will set in motion a self-discovery process that will lead you to find your special interests.

To begin, get out a pad of paper and a pen. When you take time to write your responses, rather than just think about them, you will give each question more care and consideration.

- What do you like to do? What gives you pleasure and makes you feel good?
- What interests, hobbies, or activities did you put on hold to raise your family?
- What did you enjoy doing as a child?

My Turn

- What are your skills, aptitudes, or talents? What do you feel most competent doing?
- Do you prefer working with people, information, or things?
- What do you consider your accomplishments to date?
- What do you feel is missing from your life—intellectually, emotionally, spiritually, and physically?

If answering these questions feels too structured, just dive right in and experiment. In fact, most of the women I interviewed did not use a formal inventory but developed their own method of finding and seeking their passions. When I spoke to Melanie Currie, an administrative assistant, just three months after her third and last child left for college, she had just begun questioning what she had achieved and how she might use her free time. "I have accomplished, in my eyes, raising three children to be self-sufficient, but I have never done anything just for me," she said. "What do I really want? I don't know because I never had time to think about it. I don't even know what makes me happy. A clean house? Redecorating? I'd like to get involved in some things in the community, maybe my church. I'd like to start going to the art museum, going to more concerts.

"I don't know what I'll end up doing, but I know when I say, 'I would like to do this, this, and this,' some people—like my husband—will look at me funny. Then I'll say, 'Well, I'm entitled. I'm a person too, you know.'"

Judy Kramer, on the other hand, used a process of elimination and brainstorming until she arrived at the possibility of opening a frozen yogurt shop: "Do I want to go back and get my master's and go into teaching?" she recalls asking herself. "I knew I definitely didn't want to go into the public schools and deal with all those little monsters. I had subbed for a year, but I wasn't sure I wanted to do that. Do I want to sit at a computer all day? Definitely no. Then I thought, what can I do that gives me freedom? *I do want my freedom.* I didn't want to be tied down twelve months a year. Then I came across this franchise that would be open six months a year. It seemed perfect for me: You work hard for six months, and then you have six months to do things you want."

WHO ARE WE NOW?

This is also a good time to assess your relationship with your husband. Neither of you is now constrained by your children's schedules and needs, so you're free to concentrate on yourselves as a couple. Whether you feel giddy with freedom and cram your weekends with activities or feel that your kids' leaving has left you with too much free time, it can be helpful to sit down with your husband and appraise your relationship. By considering the following areas in the same thoughtful way you assessed yourself, you will discover what you enjoy as a couple, what areas of your relationship need work, and what interests and friendships you'd like to pursue in the future.

Interests: Think back to your dating days. What did you do "way back when" that was fun? Next, consider what new interests you'd like to pursue as a couple now that you have the time. If no interests come to mind immediately, try brainstorming about activities you always wanted to do—if only you had more freedom. Would you like to join a hiking or biking club, start folk dancing every week, or listen to chamber music? Dare to break out of your routine. Do something that's totally off the wall. Whatever you choose, make a commitment to each other that you will do it—no matter what. Then keep that time open. You may be surprised at how a new interest enlivens your relationship and gives you a new appreciation of your husband.

Togetherness: Would you like more quality time as a couple? Or do you feel that you're together *too much* and that you need more space to pursue your individual interests? Find a quiet time to discuss this topic with each other. Be honest about what you need as an individual and what you'd like as a couple. Don't be surprised if you and your husband disagree. It's rare for husbands and wives to have the exact same needs for closeness and distance. Once you've aired your feelings and needs, talk in specific, concrete ways about what you can each do to feel satisfied individually and as a couple.

Friends: How do you each feel about the quantity and quality of time spent with other couples? Are you bored with your "old" friends, ready to weed out perfunctory relationships? Are you eager to meet new couples at this stage of your life? When you pursue new interests as a couple, you'll have an opportunity to meet new couples with similar interests. With the children out of the house, you'll also have more time and opportunity to develop closer relationships with your "old" friends. I was struck by the number of women who told me that only seeing couples on Saturday evenings felt unsatisfying now. They arranged to take day outings or weekend trips with other couples or just hang out together.

IS WORK STILL WORKING FOR YOU?

Whether you work for a salary or as a volunteer, how you spend your day matters. With your children gone and all the accompanying daily aggravations lessened, much of your energy will probably flow to your daytime activity. Now is the time to examine how you spend your day and whether it gives you the satisfaction you desire or whether your priorities have changed. First, evaluate your present situation by answering the following questions:

- How satisfied are you generally with how you spend your day?
- What is most rewarding for you? What percent of your day is spent doing what you enjoy?
- What is least rewarding for you? How much of your time is spent doing what you dislike?
- How do you feel about the people with whom you associate most closely?
- What causes you the most stress?
- How can you eliminate some of your stress and increase the activities you enjoy?

If you learn that you spend the majority of your time in tasks you dislike or with people who stress you out, consider altering how you spend your day. The following options are available to you, depending on your financial situation and your motivation to change:

- move from a volunteer to a paid position
- try to advance in your present place of work
- move to a new workplace
- stop working for someone else, and start working for yourself: open your own business or become a consultant
- cut back on your hours or responsibilities at the office and do more volunteer work.

GO FOR THE GOAL

You've assessed yourself, your marriage, and your daily activities. What now? Devise a plan and commit yourself to making it happen. Include short- and long-term goals. Put your plan in writing and post it in a place where you'll see it every day. Then, get started.

PACE YOUR GROWTH

You want time for your own pursuits; then force that time at first if that's what it takes to get you going. Schedule a regular morning walk with a friend, arrange to take piano lessons once a week; tell your husband that you need an hour after work to unwind and that you are not to be disturbed.

If you have a long-term goal, initiate a small shift in one area. If you aim to go to graduate school, send for several college catalogs as a starter. If you want to begin an exercise program, get an exercise book or videotape at the library, call your physician for a physical examination, or begin walking around the block. Give yourself mini-deadlines as well. If you're looking for a new job, commit yourself to making at least three inquiry calls each week. You'll find that you can break up one seemingly enormous task into smaller, more manageable goals. Reaching each one in turn will give you a well-earned sense of accomplishment, and you'll be able to see the progress you're making toward the bigger objective.

Try publicizing your commitment—it may help to keep you on track. If you tell a good friend, "I'm going to start biking every day after work," you're more likely to stick to it, because you know she'll ask how your new activity is working out the next time she speaks to you. This personal interest—call it support or motivation—can give you the extra push you need to persist with your new activity until it becomes a part of your life.

Take pride in every change you make—no matter how small. Try not to judge your actions. No one else can determine what you "should" do. In fact, others may not even notice that you've made a shift in your behavior. Remember: You are making modifications for yourself; do what feels right for you now.

The changes you make need not be permanent and certainly are not irreversible. If you begin volunteering at a shelter for battered women, for example, and decide after several weeks that the environment depresses you, move on to something else. You might need to try several types of volunteer work before you find the one that gratifies you. The moves you make are not set in stone.

Remember too that the course of progress rarely runs smoothly. You may have setbacks, meet resistance, lose faith, or feel discouraged. But as you forge ahead despite these hindrances, you will become more visible. You will revitalize yourself. And in the process, you will gain a sense of pride and power.

VISUALIZE YOUR GOAL

We all know how negative thoughts can prevent our moving ahead. The reverse is also true: Positive thoughts can motivate us. Cancer patients use visualization to imagine the good cells killing off the bad ones. Athletes use visualization to improve their performance. You can use visualization to increase the likelihood of achieving your goal.

Find a quiet spot where you feel comfortable and envision yourself taking the first step toward your goal. What are you wearing? Where are you going? Who else is there? Proceed step by step until you achieve your goal. See yourself *there*: acting in your first play for a community theater, being your own boss, or sculpting a marvelous figure. Whatever your goal, imagine all the details in technicolor. Repeat this exercise again and again.

Visualizing will help you think positively. It will keep you focused on what you can do, not on the deterrents to your progress. If you can visualize it, it can happen.

REWARD YOUR PROGRESS

When you have achieved some progress toward your goal, take time to pat yourself on the back. Savor that moment. Recognize how far you've come and how much you've achieved. Give yourself a reward, whether it's a frozen yogurt sundae, an afternoon at the beach, or a massage. Do what fits your budget and makes you feel good. We all know that "nothing succeeds like success." It feeds on itself. When you take time to appreciate your progress, you'll whet your appetite to do more. And you will.

DON'T LET THE NAYSAYERS GET THE BEST OF YOU

As you begin to make changes, prepare yourself for strong reactions from others, especially those closest to you. You may be surprised to learn that the people you counted on most cannot be there for you for reasons of their own. They may feel competitive, indifferent, or threatened.

Our husbands, in particular, can feel unsettled by changes we initiate and by the personal growth that can result. In fact, one recent study on women at midlife found that the most serious obstacle to a woman's growth was her husband's objections.[2] When Melanie Currie began going to the movies with her sister once a week, her husband made such comments as "I see you're out gallivanting around again." She tried to ignore his words, but they put a damper on her mood when she left the house. Nonetheless, she continued going because these outings were important to her.

When Susan Cohen, an artist, told her husband that she wanted to go back to school for a master's in fine arts, he was totally against it. At first he told her they couldn't afford it. But after much discussion, they arrived at his real fears: "Mark told me that he was afraid that I would become too independent and have an easier time leaving because I could then support myself," she recalls.

"I told him that going for my master's was something I really wanted to do but that I needed his help with it. He made it harder because I had to fight him. Mark had this fantasy of academic life and a fear that I'd meet some dashing professor who'd carry me away." Susan and Mark went for marital counseling while they lived through the graduate school experience, and as she went to class and came home each evening, still eager to spend time as a couple, Mark's fears began to dissipate. "My going to graduate school added to our lives, rather than taking away from them," says Susan, who today holds a university teaching job.

Our mothers, too, may have difficulty accepting our breaking out of old patterns, particularly those mothers who did not work outside the home and still maintain traditional ideas about women's roles. While they may take pride in our accomplishments, they may also believe deep down that our energy belongs at home. They may feel threatened by our success and have difficulty understanding what drives us or fear that we won't have time for them as we move ahead. These women may covertly or overtly try to thwart our progress. They may make sarcastic comments about our hectic schedule or jokes about our deserting them or show a lack of interest in our new projects.

Not all our friends are supportive either. Suppose you have a close friend whose children are the same ages as yours. As mothers, you've been through everything together: potty training, homesickness at overnight camp, teens' first dates, and departure for college. Both your children and hers have left home. You're ready to move on, but she is not—for whatever reason. While she may listen to your struggles, it may be difficult for her to wholeheartedly support your efforts because they threaten her. Your progress points up her inactivity. In truth, she'd rather not hear about what you're doing. She may convey this in subtle ways by tuning you out, cutting you off, or "forgetting" something important you said about a new project.

OVERCOMING RESISTANCE FROM OTHERS

Lack of support from the people who matter most to us can be very painful. In most cases, it stems from the other person's fear that she or he will be left behind or become less important as we move ahead. We need to forge on even if those closest to us don't like it. At the same time, we can try to ease the transition for them.

Before you make a change, whether it's as major as applying to graduate school or as simple as taking a walk every evening with a good friend, sit down and discuss it with the person who will be most affected. If it's your husband, tell him what you plan to do. Don't ask for permission or approval. He may need reassurance that you still care about him. Assure him that you're not choosing your friend over him. This is something you need to do for yourself. As you initiate more changes, he'll probably need to hear more often, "I still love you." But be sure to add, "But I need to do this for myself."

Keep your husband involved as you progress so he feels a part of your new life. Share your ups and downs with him. Seek his advice. Introduce him to new friends or colleagues. The more he feels involved in your new course, the more likely his fears will dissipate. With time, you may find he will become your strongest backer.

BUILD A STRONG SUPPORT SYSTEM

Support, women told me again and again, mattered tremendously in their efforts to change. Encouragement can come in many forms and from many different people. As you begin to make changes, evaluate carefully who will support you, what kind of assistance you need, and how to get it.

Husbands can provide enormous support. When Judy Kramer opened her frozen yogurt business, her husband put in hundreds of hours to help her get started. She remembers, "My husband was good at putting together all the mechanics to get this business going for me. He got the first store up and running, handled all the construction and that sort of thing. I did the actual hiring, and once it was open, he was hands-off. It's all mine. And the best part is, if dinner's not on the table, he couldn't care less."

Judy's children encouraged her to start the business too, saying things like, "Mom, do something for yourself." Her son, who worked for her each summer, gained a new respect for her. "We worked hard, the two of us, and I think he had a greater appreciation that mom is pretty darn capable," she said with pride. When Melanie Currie, the administrative assistant introduced earlier in this chapter, is ready to make a move, she knows her two daughters will support her. She says, "I know just what they'll say, 'Go for it, Mom. You're entitled.'"

Our friends, too, can be enormously encouraging. As role models, they can give us permission and strength to do what we fear. As confidantes, they can share our progress. To get the support you need to take risks, start an ongoing dialogue with a close friend with whom you can speak openly about your concerns and ambivalences. Or set up a buddy system with a friend who is also moving out in new ways. Check in with each other weekly; that will keep you both on track. Knowing that you will be talking to her can motivate you when you feel reluctant to take the next step. When you're feeling discouraged, her words can buoy you. And when you make progress, she will truly appreciate it, because she's struggling with similar issues.

Most of our mothers cannot be role models for this time in our lives because we live so differently from the way they did. But many of our mothers have proved to be our most faithful advocates, press agents, and cheerleaders. There may be models in other generations and branches of your families: A sister, an aunt, or a cousin may be able to serve as a positive example or as an additional support.

GETTING MORE FROM YOUR SUPPORTS

Unfortunately, most of us do not have all the support we would like. If you feel you are not receiving enough aid or the right kind from others, look carefully at yourself. Are you clear about what you want? And are you asking for it in the right way?

We often assume that the other person intuitively *knows* what we want, without our having to say it. We think: *If my husband really loves me, he should understand what I need. If he really cares about me, he'll do it without my asking.* Not true. We need to ask for what we want in a way that makes the other person receptive to giving it.

First, be clear in your own mind about what kind of support you want. Are you looking for someone to simply listen to you, or do you want him to play the devil's advocate? Do you need to talk every day or once a week? Do you feel better talking in person, or will the phone do? Or maybe you need concrete help with the laundry, cooking, or dishes or the gift of time alone.

Once you've decided what kind of support you need, ask yourself whether your husband, mother, or friend is capable of giving it to you. We cannot be all things to all people. If your best friend is going through a divorce, she may not be able to give you the kind of support you need right now. If your husband is experiencing business reversals, he may have no patience for your searching for more meaning in your life. If they can't be there for you, accept the reality and find support in other ways. But if you feel they can encourage you now, ask for what you need.

Timing is important. Choose a quiet hour when you know you will not be interrupted, not when one of you is running out the door. Be direct, specific, and clear about what you want. Use "I" messages: "I'm feeling overloaded at work this week. Would you be able to cook dinner Tuesday and Wednesday?" This communication lets him know how you are feeling and states your request. It's much more effective than saying, "You never cook. Why do I do all the work?" and hoping he'll get the message that you want him to cook. Chances are, you'll just anger him, and he'll do nothing. If you're feeling down, your request may be very simple: "I need to talk" or "I need a hug."

EXPAND YOUR NETWORK

If you cannot get the support you need from the people in your life right now, seek out those who can give it to you. Stretch your mind and think of unusual ways to network, whether you have to build your own support system or seek experts.

Create Your Own Support Group

Support groups have become a staple in our society. Groups exist for widows, for overeaters, for alcoholics, even for procrastinators. Still, you may not be able to find a support group to meet your needs right now. If that's the case, create your own. One woman told me she formed a "power group" of four people who want to make career changes. They are all in different careers, so they're not competitive. They meet once a month for lunch, and each person has 20 minutes of "on" time during which they can talk about their progress, ask for advice, or seek direction.

When I teach freelance writing, I encourage my students to exchange phone numbers on the last class so they can become "writing buddies." Although they come to class as total strangers, sharing the experience and the desire to write bonds them. Keeping in touch after the class ends will help them break the isolation of writing and get support in their new pursuit.

A friend of mine, who loves movies but feels she never sees enough, formed a movie group. Eight women go to the movies one Friday night a month and go out for coffee afterwards to discuss the films. Many women form book groups in the same way. Call a few friends who like to read; ask each of them to invite a friend whom you don't know so you can bring in new people. After three or four meetings, you'll have a core group, a mixture of old and new friends who love reading and discussing books.

Seek Professional Help

If you are thinking about a career move, you may want to talk to a career counselor who's trained to help people focus on their best options and get them on track. If you are toying with going back to school, meet with a continuing education adviser at a local college to review your choices. If you want to excel at public speaking, hire a coach. If you feel internal issues are holding you back, psychotherapy can help you get unstuck.

Time and again, women told me that getting professional help motivated them to take action. Before Susan Cohen, the artist you read about earlier in this chapter, broached the subject of applying to a master's program in fine arts with her husband, Mark, she went into psychotherapy to work out her own issues. "My therapist 'gave me permission' to go to graduate school," she remembers. "I knew I would have to go against my husband to do what I wanted. She gave me examples of how other women acted in similar situations. She also helped me get in touch with my anger about *not* doing what I wanted to do.

"My therapist became an important role model. She reflected a lot of the things I wanted to become. She empowered me to be a more complete person. I still struggle, but she helped me see what I could take for myself and gave me permission to do a lot of things I hadn't done but wanted to."

SILENCE THE NOISE IN YOUR HEAD

Sometimes we can be our own worst enemy: Our inner demons hold us back. We procrastinate, we blame ourselves, we hold others responsible. We want to be "*there,*" but we balk at taking the first steps toward getting there. Everyone has resistance in varying degrees to trying new paths. Just because someone has successfully mastered a task or achieved a goal doesn't mean that she has no internal conflicts. Rather, she has managed to confront them and overcome them to accomplish her goal.

Do you hold yourself back with self-criticism? When we blame ourselves, we are less likely to embark on a new activity because we focus on our limitations and ignore our strengths. Do you find yourself saying, "I should be content with what I have" or "I shouldn't be feeling this way"? Or maybe you tell yourself, "This should be easier." Your self-critique implies that it *would* be easier if only you were smarter/quicker/more savvy, etc. Therefore, it's *your* fault that you don't possess the positive traits needed to move ahead.

If this thinking pattern sounds familiar, try to focus on your strengths and your achievements. Replace negative messages with positive ones. Remind yourself of how you mastered other obstacles in the past. I've used this technique myself many times when I've felt blocked while writing: when I thought I didn't know how to organize my material, or I couldn't express on paper the jumble in my head, or I felt so overwhelmed that I couldn't focus on the chapter at hand. When I get "stuck" like this, I often reread a piece of my writing that I'm particularly proud of or page through one of my earlier books. This process reminds me: Yes, I *can* write. I've written other books, so I *can*—and I will—complete this one too.

Are you still blaming yourself for being the victim—of a bad childhood, an abusive marriage, demanding children? Is "I *can't* . . ." a familiar refrain of yours? Victimhood creates self-pity yet points the finger at someone else as the cause. Acting as a victim breeds inertia, making you feel helpless and hopeless. Instead, try to keep the past in the past. Reframe your situation by focusing on the stamina you developed to survive a horrendous experience. This strength will serve you well now.

Do you still blame yourself for a son's or daughter's emotional problems or difficulties? Continuing to do so can inhibit you from moving on with your own life and may prevent your children from taking responsibility for themselves—because you're doing it for them. Try to forgive yourself for whatever you feel you've done. Reread chapter three and recount all the other influences, besides your mothering, that affected your children. When you forgive yourself, both you and your children will be able to progress with your lives.

Are you blaming someone else for your own inactivity? If you feel unsupported in making changes, you're probably angry. Sure, it's easier to lash out—at our husbands, our mothers, our kids— than to take responsibility ourselves. But that won't get you where you want to go. Instead, reread the sections on getting more support from others and expanding your support system. Try to put these suggestions into practice. You'll feel much better when you claim control and take action.

IF YOU'RE STILL STUCK

If you don't feel ready to make changes yet, for any or all of the reasons already discussed, don't get discouraged. This is not a one-time opportunity. Most of us still have many years ahead and should have plenty of time to explore interests, develop second and even third careers, and create more intimacy in our relationships. Be patient with yourself, and try to accept that you're not ready yet.

However, if you sincerely want to get moving *now* but feel stuck, consider that some of the following issues may be holding you back:

Too Many Shoulds and Musts. If you find yourself constantly saying, "I should do this" or "I must do that," try to throw away the scripts, the parental and societal dictums, that probably governed much of your life. "Always in the back of my mind there's this voice telling me, 'I shouldn't be doing this,'" said a woman who opened her own business after her children left for college. "*They* (her family) should come first. It's really a hard pattern to break—that's the most irritating part of this."

Replace the old scripts with the following new ones: You are not selfish when you take care of yourself. It's all right to be assertive, even aggressive. Everything you do doesn't have to be perfect. Let these be your mantras. They will help you concentrate on what *you* want to do and on what makes *you* feel good.

Saying "I Can't" Too Often. No matter how life has treated us, we always have a choice about how we act and react. Learn to say "I can" or "I will" or "I deserve to . . . ." It will energize you and transform you from a helpless victim to a powerful actor. Psychologist Charlotte Davis Kasl agrees. "It's crucial that you avoid saying 'I can't' rather than thinking of the choices you do have," she writes in her book *Finding Joy*. "'I can't' throws up a roadblock in the mind and stops your creativity and flow of energy."[3]

Trying to Change the Unchangeable. How many times have you said to yourself, "We'd have such a great marriage with the kids gone if only my husband would stop drinking" or "I'd be so happy if only Jeff were better adjusted at college" or "I'd feel free to concentrate on myself if I weren't so worried about Susie not getting married." In each of these "if only" statements, you base your happiness on someone else making changes in his or her life. The truth is, however, that we cannot change anyone except ourselves. Try to accept what you cannot change and work on what you can change: yourself.

Lack of Support. You want to get your master's degree, but your husband insists you help him at the office, or your mother needs you to take her to the grocery store, or your children still call every other day from college to discuss their problems. No one seems to support your developing a life of your own. If this sounds familiar, take stock. Consider who is actually holding you back. Are you saying "I can't" when you truly do have other options? Are you blaming someone else when the responsibility for your inaction lies with you? If you feel you can't shift gears without your family's blessings, then follow the steps suggested earlier for getting more support from them or putting yourself in a more nurturing environment.

Unrealistic Expectations. Perhaps you have already signed up for an acting class and are working on the sets for a community theater, yet you still feel dissatisfied. Or maybe you've yearned to paint for years, but the class at the local art center is not as enriching as you had hoped. Perhaps you are expecting too much too soon. You have spent almost twenty years putting your needs on the back burner while you nurtured others. It will take time to feel comfortable taking care of yourself and to find activities that match your needs. Learn to slow down and savor your time, to allow your creativity to flow. Be patient with yourself. Try to enjoy what you are doing now. Your interests may need time to grow.

IF YOUR CHILDREN HAVEN'T LEFT HOME YET . . .

If your children are still in high school, you are in the enviable position of being able to prepare yourself for their departure. If you have the time and resources to begin thinking about yourself and your needs while your children are still at home, you can ease your transition from active parenting to the postparental period.

My Turn

Can you truly prepare though? Bonnie Hoffman, a journalist and the mother of Lisa, now 26, and Stacy, 24, told me that one night when the family sat around the dinner table shortly before Lisa left for college, Stacy said to Lisa: "Leave the room so we can see what it feels like when you're gone." They all roared. Stacy had expressed in concrete terms her apprehensions about how the family dynamics would change with Lisa's departure. Could they prepare themselves by having Lisa leave the room? Of course not, but when Stacy verbalized her concerns and the family had a good laugh, they all acknowledged that their life at home would change with the absence of one member.

Perhaps Bonnie could have used this opportunity to open a family discussion about Lisa's departure. You have this opportunity too. Discuss what might be different at home without one child, how the dynamics might change, and your hopes and expectations for the family in the future. Don't burden your child who is leaving with all your emotions about her impending departure, but a brief acknowledgment by you that things will be different at home may allow all the family members to verbalize some of their unspoken concerns.

Jungian psychotherapist Verena Kast recommends that parents do "memory work" with their children before they leave home. She suggests that we reflect on our lives with our children and recall the qualities—both positive and negative—they evoked in us through the years. For example, an infant elicits tenderness. Playing in the sandbox helps us get in touch with our childlike qualities. "We can reexplore the past in everyday conversation when young people ask about their early childhood," she writes. "We can reiterate the qualities that the other person evokes; we can talk about what is left behind and cannot be lost." If you have younger children still at home, make these conversations a common ritual while they are growing up as a way to prepare them and you for the time when you really say goodbye.[4]

Talk to close friends, particularly those whose children have already left home or are about to leave, about your feelings. Your friends' support can help you feel less abandoned and less alone, particularly if you're a single parent. For married women, share your feelings with your husband and plan for your future as a couple. Such discussions will lend support and help you anticipate the future with joy.

Connie Kowalski, a 54-year-old nurse, might have adjusted more easily to her youngest son's departure if she had someone with whom to discuss her feelings the summer before David left for college. Connie told me that she cried "half the summer" but didn't realize until months later why she wept so much. "I wasn't thinking about his leaving," she said. "Something would happen, and I would just cry. David was more difficult to prepare than his brother. I couldn't get him organized, so I was so frustrated, trying to get him to do the things that I thought he should. Two days before he left, I wanted to buy him jeans because he only had one pair, and I couldn't picture him out there without any clothes. He said to me, 'I'm fine, I'm OK, I don't need anything else.' Then I started crying—the first time I cried in front of him. He looked at me funny and gave me a hug. Then he went shopping with me. But when he left, I was okay. I did all my crying that summer."

Connie may convince herself that she's okay, but when I spoke with her in December, four months after David left home, she wept through the entire interview. She felt embarrassed and apologized profusely, insisting that "everything is really fine now." Perhaps if Connie had shared her feelings with her friends or husband before her son left and during the early months, she would be more accepting of her emotions and have less need to deny them.

As with any loss, you cannot prepare yourself totally. But if you initiate some of the strategies suggested earlier in this chapter while your youngest child is in high school, you may experience a smoother transition into the postparental period. You can begin making yourself a priority while your children are still at home. Start the self-assessment process now instead of waiting until they leave. If you have the time, explore new activities or pursue interests you set aside to raise your children.

Rita Lynchberg, a divorced paralegal, prepared in earnest when her three children were teenagers. "When they got into their teen years, I pretty well realized that one day they would not be here. So I very consciously and very actively made sure I had hobbies," she said. "I was preparing ahead of time, because I knew it would be a very hard awakening when they left. When the last one went off to college, it was not really that terrible."

Rita joined a softball league, took cooking lessons, subscribed to a theater series, and expanded her vegetable garden. She even bought a piano and learned how to play. She pursued all these activities for about three years. Her busyness helped her get through the initial transition. But after awhile, she felt *too* busy. Now, with her children gone almost six years, she has abandoned some of her early activities and concentrates only on what gives her pleasure. When she's not working, she loves playing the piano and tending her garden. "I've become an organic farmer. I make my own compost. When the circus comes to town, I go down to get the elephant dung," she says laughing. "I grow so many vegetables. All summer long I bring in bags of potatoes and tomatoes to the people at work. They love it. And so do I."

SEIZING YOUR TURN

It has often been said there are only two lasting bequests we can give our children—one is roots; the other, wings. The same adage could be applied to ourselves: Most of us have planted our roots deep in our families. We've perpetuated our cultural and religious traditions. We've shared our values, our cares, our concerns, and of course, our love. We've given our hearts to our sons and daughters.

In giving our children roots, parenting has grounded us, too. It has taught us what truly matters. We've learned patience and tolerance, humility and acceptance. Our children have broadened us and frustrated us. They have enraged us and thrilled us. Our connection, still so important and so powerful, binds us to our sons and daughters no matter where they live or what they do.

Now, with our children on their own, each of us has an opportunity to try our wings. We may hover close to home until we gain confidence or soar, assured and free. We may coast languidly until we hit turbulence or venture boldly into uncharted skies. Whatever your course, enjoy it. "Be here now," the yoga masters tell us. Yes, set goals; certainly, strive for them. But remember that meaning is in the moment and pleasure is in the process. Treasure your turn.

NOTES

CHAPTER ONE

1. Bart (1967); E. Deykin, et al. (1966); Jacobson & Klerman (1966); Weissman & Paykel (1974).
2. Rubin, p. 15.
3. Radloff, p. 780.
4. *Philadelphia Inquirer*, January 4, 1995, p. H1.
5. Greer, pp. 20–21.
6. Greer, p. 25.
7. Levinson, p. 4.
8. Colarusso, p. 109.
9. Levinson, back cover.
10. Levinson, p. 109.
11. Levinson, p. 195.
12. Gilligan, p. 12.
13. Jordan, Kaplan, Miller, Stiver, Surrey, pp. 208–9.
14. Friedan, p. 146.
15. Goodman, Ellen, *Philadelphia Inquirer*, 1986.
16. U.S. Department of Labor, Bureau of Labor Statistics, Current Population Survey, March 1988.
17. Families and Work Institute, 1993. This 1992 longitudinal study surveyed almost 3,000 employed men and women with families and asked them to assess the person they felt took major responsibility at home.
18. Black & Hill, p. 288.
19. Gutmann, pp. 212–13.
20. Gutmann, p. 156. This study by Marjorie Lowenthal, Majda Thurnher, and David Chiriboga surveyed middle-aged urban American couples in 1975.
21. Hollis, pp. 43–44.

CHAPTER TWO

1. Llewelyn and Osborne, p. 165.
2. Lazarre, p. 152.
3. Chessick, p. 19.
4. Lazarre, back cover.
5. Lazarre, p. 27.

6. Swigart, p. 114.
7. Chodorow, p. 7.
8. Families and Work Institute, 1993.
9. Lazarre, p. 62.
10. Chodorow, p. 207.
11. Jong, pp. 307–8.
12. *Philadelphia Inquirer,* May 7, 1994, p. D1.
13. Lowinsky, p. 3.
14. Nadelson and Notman, p. 24.
15. Block, p. 182.
16. Raphael-Leff, pp. 151–68.
17. Ibid.

CHAPTER THREE

1. Rubin, p. 23.
2. Ibid., p. 38.
3. Ibid.
4. Ibid., p. 23.
5. Hollis, p. 29.
6. Swigart, p. 6.
7. Hancock, p. 151.
8. Llewelyn & Osborne, p. 163.
9. Caplan & Hall-McCorquodale, pp. 345–53.
10. Llewelyn & Osborne, p. 163.
11. Caplan & Hall-McCorquodale, pp. 345–53.
12. Swigart, p. 221.
13. Birns, pp. 1–19.
14. Viorst, p. 241.
15. Birns, pp. 1–19.
16. Shapiro, pp. 46–47.
17. Sandmaier, p. 46.
18. Ibid.
19. Young and Haynie, pp. 59–65.
20. Ibid.
21. Klein and Gotti., p. 32.
22. Quindlen, *New York Times,* June 19, 1994, p. 21.
23. Viorst, p. 239.
24. Viorst, p. 240.

CHAPTER FOUR

1. Kast, pp. 30–34.
2. Swigart, p. 186.
3. Goodman, *Philadelphia Inquirer*, Sept. 17, 1986.
4. Bassoff, 1994, p. 5.
5. Bassoff, 1994, p. 65.
6. Bassoff, 1994, p. 67.
7. Bassoff, 1994, p. 224.
8. Miller, pp. 79–80.
9. La Sorsa and Fodor, pp. 593–605.
10. Hancock, p. 147.
11. Bassoff, 1989, p. 217.
12. Bassoff, 1994, p. 214.
13. Bassoff, 1994, p. 230.
14. Bassoff, 1994, pp. 230–31.
15. McGoldrick, pp. 269–81.
16. Lerner, 1985, p. 86.
17. Lerner, 1985, p. 81.
18. Lerner, 1989, p. 27.
19. Friday, pp. 461–62.
20. Volkan and Zintl, p. 5.

CHAPTER FIVE

1. Lerner, 1989, p. 3.
2. Bassoff, 1994, pp. 224–26.
3. Greenberg, p. 149.
4. Rhodes, p. 17.
5. Monthly Vital Statistics Report, Vol. 43, No. 9, Supplement, March 22, 1995.
6. Lerner, 1989, pp. 143–61.
7. Roberts and Newton, p. 158.
8. Lowenthal, pp. 10–14.
9. Apter, p. 302.
10. Apter, p. 305.
11. Rubin, 1985, pp. 133–35.
12. O'Connor, p. 56.
13. Jong, p. 103.

My Turn

CHAPTER SIX

1. Meyer, pp. 3–17.
2. Gilligan, p. 159.
3. Rubin, p. 55.
4. Hancock, p. 25; Prose, p. 23.
5. Burka and Yuen, p. 21.
6. Tresemer, pp. 32–36.
7. Tresemer, pp. 17–18.
8. All of this preceding section from Jeffers, pp. 21–30.
9. Bateson, p. 16.
10. *New York Times*, September 15, 1993.

CHAPTER SEVEN

1. Johnston, pp. 156–57.
2. Roberts and Newton, p. 158.
3. Kasl, p. 115.
4. Kast, pp. 41–46.

BIBLIOGRAPHY

Apter, Terri. *Secret Paths: Women in the New Midlife*. New York: W. W. Norton, 1995.

Bardwick, Judith M. *In Transition: How Feminism, Sexual Liberation, and Search for Self-Fulfillment Have Altered Our Lives*. New York: Holt, Rhinehart and Winston, 1979.

Barnett, Roslyn, and Grace Baruch. "Women in the Middle Years: A Critique of Research and Theory." *Journal of Women Quarterly*, 1988.

Barnett, Roslyn, Grace Baruch, and Caryl Rivers. *Life Prints: New Patterns of Love and Work for Today's Women*. New York: McGraw-Hill, 1983.

Bart, Pauline B. "Depression in Middle-Aged Women: Some Socioloculcural Factors." doctoral dissertation, University of California, Los Angeles, 1967.

Baruch, Grace, and Jeanne Brooks-Gunn, eds. *Women in Mid-Life*. New York and London: Plenum Press, 1984.

Bassoff, Evelyn. *Between Mothers and Sons: The Making of Vital and Loving Men*. New York: Dutton Books, 1994.

————. *Mothers and Daughters: Loving and Letting Go*. New York: Plume, 1989.

Bateson, Mary Catherine. *Composing a Life*. New York: Plume, 1990.

Belencky, Mary Field, Blythe McVicker Clinchy, Nancy Rule Goldberger, and Jill Mattuck Tarule. *Women's Ways of Knowing*. New York: Basic Books, 1986.

Benedek, Therese. "Parenthood as a Developmental Phase: A Contribution to Libido Theory." *Journal of the American Psychoanalytic Association*, 2, no. 3 (1959): 389–417.

Birns, Beverly. "The Mother-Infant Tie: Fifty Years of Theory, Science and Science Fiction." Work in Progress, The Stone Center, Wellesley College, Wellesley, Mass., no. 21 (1985).

Black, Sionag M., and Clara E. Hill. "The Psychological Well-Being of Women in the Middle Years." *Psychology of Women Quarterly*, 8, no. 3 (spring 1984): 282–92.

My Turn

Blaker, Karen. *Celebrating 50: Women Share Their Experiences, Challenges, and Insights on Becoming 50.* Chicago: Contemporary Books, 1990.

Block, Joyce. *Motherhood as Metamorphosis.* New York: Dutton, 1990.

Borland, Delores Cabic. "A Cohort Analysis Approach to the Empty Nest Syndrome Among Three Ethnic Groups of Women: A Theoretical Position." *Journal of Marriage and the Family* (February 1982): 117–29.

Brown, Lyn Mikel, and Carol Gilligan. *Meeting at the Crossroads: Women's Psychology and Girl's Development.* Cambridge, Mass., and London, England: Harvard University Press, 1992.

Burka, Jane B., and Lenora M. Yuen. *Procrastination: Why You Do It, What To Do About It.* Reading, Mass.: Addison-Wesley, 1983.

Caine, Lynn. *What Did I Do Wrong?* New York: Arbor House, 1985.

Caplan, Paula J., and Ian Hall-McCorquodale. "Mother-Blaming in Major Clinical Journals." *American Journal of Orthopsychiatry*, 55, no. 2 (1985): 345–53.

_____. "The Scapegoating of Mothers: A Call for Change," *American Journal of Orthopsychiatry*, 55, no. 4 (October 1985): 610–13.

Chessick, Richard. *A Dictionary for Psychotherapists.* Northvale, NJ: Jason Aronson, 1993.

Chodorow, Nancy. *The Reproduction of Mothering.* Berkeley: University of California Press, 1978.

Claremont de Castillejo, Irene. *Knowing Woman: A Feminine Psychology.* Boston and Shaftesbury: Shambhala, 1990.

Cobrun, Karen Levin, and Madge Lawrence Treeger. *Letting Go: A Parents' Guide to Today's College Experience.* Bethesda, Md.: Adler & Adler, 1988.

Colarusso, Calvin A. *Child and Adult Development: A Psychoanalytic Introduction for Clinicians.* New York and London: Plenum Press, 1992.

Deykin, E., S. Jacobson, G. Klerman, and N. Solomon. "The Empty Nest: Psychosocial Aspects of Conflicts Between Depressed Women and Their Grown Children." *American Journal of Psychiatry*, no. 122 (1966): 1422–26.

Fishel, Elizabeth. *Family Lives: What Our Children's Lives Reveal About Ourselves.* Boston: Houghton Mifflin, 1991.

Friedan, Betty. *The Fountain of Age.* New York: Simon and Schuster, 1993.

Friday, Nancy. *My Mother/My Self.* New York: Dell, 1987.

Genevie, Louis, and Eva Margolies. *The Motherhood Report: How Women Feel About Being Mothers.* New York: Macmillan, 1987.

Giele, Janet Zollinger, ed. *Women in the Middle Years: Current Knowledge and Directions for Research and Policy.* New York: John Wiley & Sons, 1982.

Gilligan, Carol. *In a Different Voice.* Cambridge, Mass.: Harvard University Press, 1982.

Greenberg, Vivian. *Children of a Certain Age.* New York: Lexington Books, 1994.

Greer, Germaine. *The Change.* New York: Alfred A. Knopf, 1992.

Gutmann, David. *Reclaimed Powers.* New York: Basic Books, 1987.

Hancock, Emily. *The Girl Within.* New York: E. P. Dutton, 1989.

Hollis, James. *The Middle Passage: From Misery to Meaning in Midlife.* Toronto, Canada: Inner City Books, 1993.

Ibsen, Henrik. *Ghosts and Three Other Plays by Henrik Ibsen.* Translated by Michael Meyer. Garden City, N.Y.: Anchor Books, 1966.

Jacobson, Shirley, and Gerald L. Klerman. "Interpersonal Dynamics of Hospitalized Depressed Patients' Home Visits." *Journal of Marriage and the Family,* 28 (1966): 94–102.

Jeffers, Suzanne. *Feel the Fear and Do It Anyway.* New York: Fawcett Columbine, 1987.

Johnston, Tracy. *Shooting the Boh.* New York: Vintage Books, 1992.

Jong, Erica. *Fear of Fifty.* New York: HarperCollins, 1994.

Jordan, Judith V., Alexandra G. Kaplan, Jean Baker Miller, Irene P. Stiver, and Janet L. Surrey. *Women's Growth in Connection: Writings from the Stone Center.* New York and London: The Guilford Press, 1991.

Josselson, Ruthellen. *Finding Herself: Pathways to Identity Development in Women.* San Francisco: Jossey-Bass Publishers, 1987.

Kasl, Charlotte Davis. *Finding Joy: 101 Ways to Free Your Spirit and Dance with Life.* New York: HarperCollins, 1994.

MY TURN

Kast, Verena. *Letting Go and Finding Yourself*. New York: Continuum, 1994.

Kerber, Linda K., Catherine G. Greeno, Eleanor E. Maccoby, Zella Luria, Carol B. Stack, and Carol Gilligan. "On *In A Different Voice*: An Interdisciplinary Forum." *Signs: Journal of Women in Culture and Society*, 2, no. 2 (1986): 304–33.

Klein, Carol, and Richard Gotti. *Overcoming Regret: Lessons from the Road Not Taken*. New York: Bantam Books, 1992.

LaSorsa, Valerie A., and Iris G. Fodor. "Adolescent Daughter/Midlife Mother Dyad: A New Look at Separation and Self-Definition." *Psychology of Women Quarterly*, 14 (1990): 593–606.

Lazarre, Jane. *The Mother Knot*. Boston: Beacon Press, 1976.

Lerner, Harriet. *The Dance of Anger*. New York: Harper & Row, 1985.

_____. *The Dance of Intimacy*. New York: Harper & Row, 1989.

"Letting Go: Why It's Hard to Let Children Grow Up." *Redbook* (May 1980): 42, 44.

Levinson, Daniel. *The Seasons of a Man's Life*. New York: Ballantine Books, 1978.

Llewelyn, Sue, and Kate Osborne. *Women's Lives*. London and New York: Routledge, 1990.

Lowenthal, M., and D. Chiriboga. "Transition to the Empty Nest: Crisis, Challenge or Relief?" *Archives of General Psychiatry*, no. 26 (1972): 8–14.

Lowenthal, Marjorie Fiske. "41 Variations Across the Adult Life Course." *The Second Stage*, 15, no. 1 (February 1975).

Lowinsky, Naomi Ruth. *Stories from the Motherline: Reclaiming the Mother-Daughter Bond, Finding our Feminine Souls*. Los Angeles: Jeremy Tarcher, 1992.

Maynard, Joyce. *Domestic Affairs: Enduring the Pleasures of Motherhood and Family Life*. New York: Times Books, 1987.

McGoldrick, Monica, John K. Pearce, and Joseph Giordano, eds. *Ethnicity and Family Therapy*. New York and London: The Guilford Press, 1982.

McLanahan, S., and J. Adams. "Parenthood and Psychological Well-Being." *Annual Review of Immunology*, 5 (1987): 237–57.

Miller, Jean Baker. *Toward a New Psychology of Women*. Boston: Beacon Press, 1976.

Miller, Sue. *For Love*. New York: HarperCollins, 1993.

Nadelson, Carol, and Malkah Notman. *The Woman Patient: Vol. 2: Concepts of Femininity and the Life Cycle*. New York: Plenum Press, 1982.

Neugarten, Bernice. *Middle Age and Aging*. Chicago: University of Chicago Press, 1968.

_____. "Dynamics of Transition of Middle Age to Old Age." *Journal of Geriatric Psychiatry*, 4, no. 1 (fall 1970).

Norman, William H., and Thomas J. Scaramella, eds. *Mid-Life: Developmental and Clinical Issues*. New York: Brunner/Magee, Publishers, 1980.

O'Connor, Pat. *Friendship Between Women: A Critical Review*. New York and London: The Guilford Press, 1992.

Peck, Teresa A. "Women's Self-Definition in Adulthood: From a Different Model?" *Psychology of Women Quarterly*, 10, 1986: 274–84.

Posner, Judith. *The Feminine Mistake: Women, Work and Identity*. New York: Warner Books, 1992.

Prose, Francine. "Confident at 11, Confused at 16." *New York Times Magazine* (January 7, 1990): 22–23, 37–39, 45–46.

Quindlen, Anna. "Fall From the Nest," *New York Times* (June 19, 1994): 21.

Radloff, Lenore Sawyer. "Depression and the Empty Nest." *Sex Roles*, 6, no. 6 (1980): 775–81.

Raphael-Leff, Joan. "Facilitators and Regulators: Vulnerability to Post-Natal Disturbance." *Journal of Psychosomatic Obstetrics and Gynecology*, 4 (1985): 151–68.

Reese, Deborah Frankel. "The Children Are Gone." *New York Times* (December 1985).

Rhodes, Dr. Sonya, with Susan Schneider. *Second Honeymoon: A Pioneering Guide for Reviving the Mid-Life Marriage*. New York: William Morrow & Co., 1992.

Rich, Adrienne. *Of Woman Born*. New York: W. W. Norton & Co., 1976.

My Turn

Roberts, Priscilla, and Peter M. Newton. "Levinsonian Studies of Women's Adult Development." *Psychology and Aging*, 2, no. 2 (1987): 154–63.

Rountree, Cathleen. *On Women Turning 50*. New York: HarperCollins, 1993.

Rusk, Tom, and Randy Read. *I Want to Change But I Don't Know How!* Los Angeles: Price Stern Sloan, 1978.

Rubin, Lillian. *Women of a Certain Age*. New York: Harper and Row, 1979.

Sandmaier, Marian. *Original Kin: The Search for Connection Among Adult Brothers and Sisters*. New York: Dutton, 1994.

Sangiuliano, Iris. *In Her Time*. New York: William Morrow, 1978.

Seligman, Martin E. P. *What You Can Change and What You Can't*. New York: Alfred A. Knopf, 1994.

Shapiro, Patricia Gottlieb. *A Parent's Guide to Childhood and Adolescent Depression*. New York: Dell, 1994.

Shapiro, Pat, and Joan Jeruchim. *Women, Mentors, and Success*. New York: Fawcett Columbine, 1992.

Sheehy, Gail. *Passages*. New York: Dutton, 1974, 1976.

_____.*The Silent Passage*. New York: Random House, 1991.

_____. *New Passages: Mapping Your Life Across Time*. New York: Random House, 1995.

Shreve, Anita. *Remaking Motherhood*. New York: Viking Penguin, 1987.

Simon, Sidney. *Getting Unstuck: Breaking Through Your Barriers to Change*. Warner Books, 1988.

Swigart, Jane. *The Myth of the Bad Mother: Emotional Realities of Mothering*. New York: Doubleday, 1991.

Tresemer, David Ward. *Fear of Success*. New York: Plenum Press, 1977.

Viorst, Judith. *Necessary Losses*. New York: Fawcett Gold Medal, 1986.

Volkan, Vamik D., and Elizabeth Zintl. *Life After Loss*. New York: Charles Scribner's Sons, 1993.

Youniss, James, and Denise L. Haynie. "Friendship in Adolescence." *Developmental and Behavioral Pediatrics*, 13, no. 1, (February 1992): 59–65.

Walker, Betty, and Marilyn Mehr. *The Courage to Change*. New York: Simon and Schuster, 1992.

INDEX